INSCAPE

2020

WASHBURN UNIVERSITY
Department of English
1700 SW College Ave
Topeka, KS 66621

Thanks to the Washburn University Department of English.

Vol. 43

inscapemagazine.org

washburn.edu/inscape

facebook.com/inscapemagazine

Cover Art: The Dreamer Finds a Blue Flower by Stephen Linsteadt

Inscape, compiled annually at Washburn University in Topeka, Kansas, features poetry, fiction, nonfiction, and visual art from the region and beyond.

INSCAPE
2020

Contents

EDITORS' CHOICE

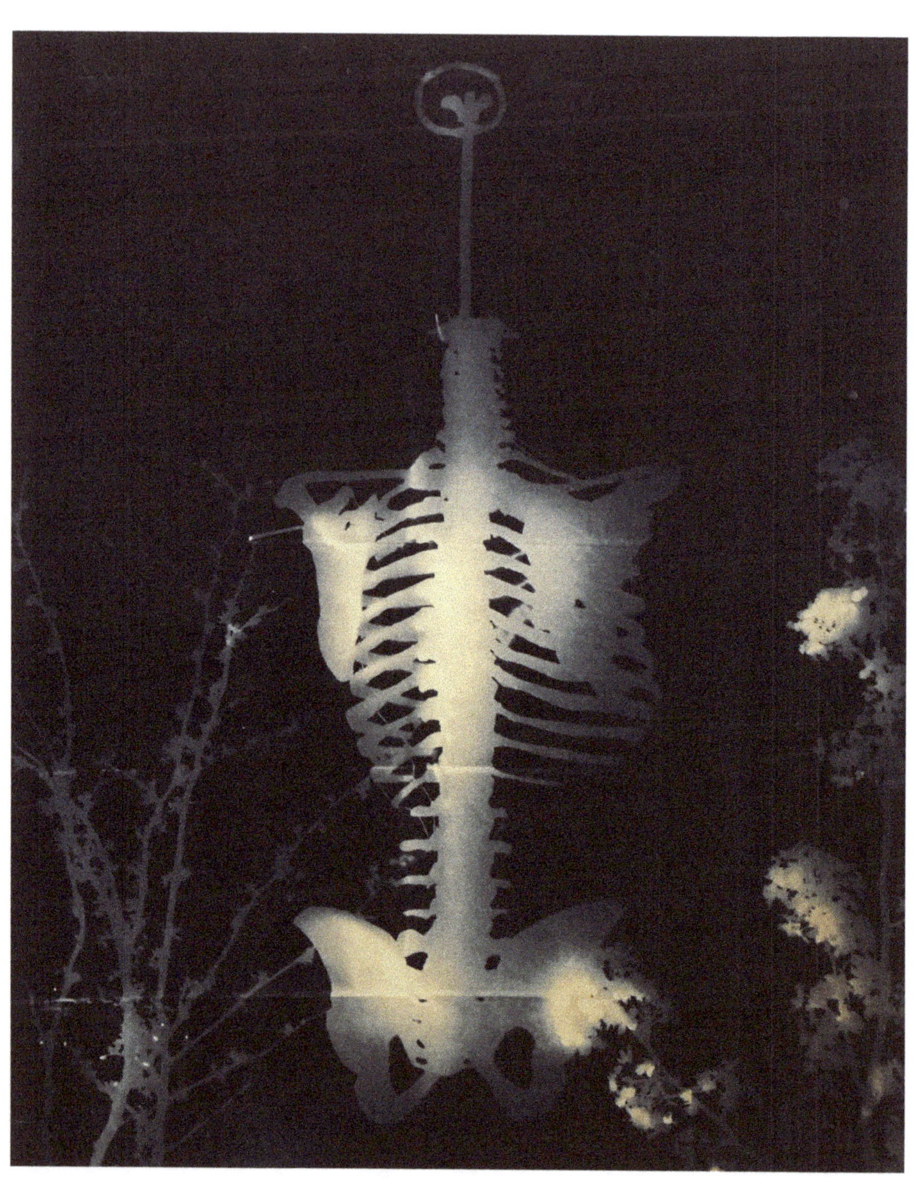

MEMENTO MORI
Harvey Flowers
Medium: Cyanotype on cotton
Dimensions: 5 x 4 feet

AFTER THE CHAINSAW ACCIDENT

Geo. Staley

I sit alone for 20 minutes
on the crinkly white paper of the
examining table at the Dr.'s office
    gashed left foot lost
    in brown antiseptic solution.

Others, if sitting in my place, may wonder

    What if I'd cut my toes off?
    Why didn't the gash bleed?
    Did I cut tendons as well as bone?
    Will I be able to run?
    How could I be so stupid?

These occur to me, though mostly
I marvel at how effortlessly, painlessly,
the chain saw in my hands tore through
running shoe, running sock, skin, and bone
and stopped
as if I'd thought, beforehand,
    How deep can I go before
    I do serious damage?

PORTRAIT OF CHRONIC PAIN AS AN INSECT

RK Taylor

crawling under skin, or instead
tent-trapped and humming
a sordid song, a funeral
march for someone
not yet dead.

evading swats from sweaty palm, i listen
as you justify my existence,
convince yourself
of my ecological import. yet still
i sense how you want me

out, feel your fear
pulse through my antenna,
hear your mutters summoning strength.

squash me, though i won't cease.
my life may be brief
and fragile, but there are many
like me. new ones each day.
only you must persist
our daily resurgence.
so before you lift me by my limbs,
leading me to scurry into your down

sleeping bag where i'll lay dormant
for the moment, know:
i'll return tomorrow
albeit in a newfangled form.

alas, i'll wait
for the final act of our mutually assured
misery, for you to find the courage
to separate our symbiotic struggle,
for you to find safety
in my slaughter.

LAKEVIEW CEMETARY

Kristin Bryant Rajan

Each morning
I run the gentle hills of Lakeview Cemetery,
a sanctuary in Cleveland, Ohio.
Statues look over me—
black tears streak stone faces,
sculpted gowns lifted and frozen in the sun.

Surrounded by dawn
and one hundred year old elm and oak,
I feel my life.
I breathe
my breath.
One with the wind,
I celebrate the morning.

Surrounded by names and dates of those departed,
I flow into energy beneath form,
I flow into the gratitude of now.

I am
the graceful stone goddesses
crying dark tears
of joy.

FLORENCE AND FIONA
Meredith Field
Medium: Acrylic
Dimensions: 11 x 14 oval

A WHISPER THROUGH THE WINTER WINDS

Trevor Oattes

My mother always told me that I was a child of winter. I suppose it started from a young age. There are pictures and home videos of me as little more than a toddler, leaping into snowbanks and carving out tiny snow angels in my little neon-blue snowsuit. When my sisters and brother – summer children, all of them – would beg my parents to return home so they could envelop themselves in blankets and gorge themselves on hot chocolate, I would remain indignant, refusing to leave my frosty playground behind.

Even throughout adolescence, I was obsessed with the winter landscape. I loved the beauty of the dancing snow flickering through the air, the way my small town landscape became entombed in soft, billowing white. When I was seven years old and stuck inside with the flu – missing a perfect snowy December afternoon, mind you – I discovered my grandfather's old 35mm film camera tucked between dusty packing boxes. It felt sturdy between my hands, like some old treasure. As soon as the flu left me I took my new prize outside and began taking photos of my frigid wonderland.

Leafless branches silhouetted against the evening sun, an unflowing frozen river beneath an old stone bridge, a red squirrel peaking its head out from a hole in a tree. The scenes that I had always loved but had never had the chance to properly express to my friends or family.

It was around this time that I met the Something.

Even now, after all these long years, I can still remember everything that happened that day. I had been out in the small birch woods behind my parents' house, nine years old and filled with glee. The first snowfall of the year had graced us the night before, signifying the dying breath of a tyrannical summer. Armed with my trusty camera I had rushed out the door, my parents yelling at me through the kitchen window so that I would stay close to the house. But it was useless; the gentle snowfall intoxicated me, and within minutes I was out of sight of my house.

The birch trees were barren and cracked, standing like emaciated giants far above me. Stepping into the woods felt like stepping into a painting. Out of the corner of my eye I saw a winter hare dart by. I aimed my camera, readying the perfect shot. But I stopped myself. I had taken plenty of pictures of hares before. No, I needed something better. This was the first shot of the season, after all. It had to be special.

Decked out in green snowsuit and boots, I was most certainly not blending in with my surroundings. Everywhere I went I saw hares and squirrels and even a few deer rushing away from me as if their lives depended on it. My young mind couldn't help but take it personally: Disney movies had led me to believe that animals were much friendlier than this. To my continued confusion, I saw a panicked squirrel run towards me, dart around my legs, and continue into the forest. Looking back, I can't believe how I didn't see the signs.

Like a fool, I decided to explore the area where the animals were running from. Pushing branches from my face, I stepped into a clearing in the woods.

And then I saw it.

The most beautiful winter landscape I had ever encountered.

I stood on the shoreline of the river that flowed behind my home. The sun hung low overhead, as if it were still working up the energy to finish rising. From where I stood I could see the shore covered in perfect, untouched snow. Birch trees stood to my left and right, framing my peripheral with their skeletal grey branches and bone-white flesh. Before me stood the frozen river, almost entirely still beneath the blue-gray ice. Only a patch of the river still revealed the running water beneath the ice, having been melted away by the lazy sun. The exposed water rippled with the sun's shining light, presenting me with the finishing touch to a perfectly composed photo of whites, blues, and oranges.

The beauty of that simple scene left me breathless, and without a thought I raised my camera, adjusted the dials and took the shot. I didn't take another; I knew it was perfect. For a few moments I just stood before this gift of nature, my youthful mind completely devoid of anything else. It took the sound of snapping branches to break me out of my trance.

The sound had surprised me. I blinked my dry eyes a few times, turning away from my landscape. Behind me stood the entire birch forest, tall and immense. Though the woods had welcomed me earlier, I now felt uneasy looking at the maze of trees. I felt the hairs at the base of my neck creep up.

I saw movement out of the corner of my eye. I thought I had seen one of the trees move. I gasped out loud, taking a step backward toward the river. I kept my eyes glued on the woods. Nothing else moved.

A cold wind blew across the ground, drifting with it the billowy top layer of snow. I felt that cold in my bones. To tell you the truth, I still do to this day.

I took a few steps forward and stopped. Everything in my head told me not to go further, not to go back into the woods. But the shoreline that I stood upon was narrow; the only other way home would be across the ice.

After minutes of panicked pondering, I forced myself to remember the beauty of the woods. The birch trees, which now looked as if they were jagged bones of the earth, were also the backdrop to so many happy childhood memories. The woods had been the setting for making snowmen with my sisters and brother, sledding, igloos, and of course my photography. With all the resolve I could muster, I shoved down the fear and stepped forward, though the hair on my neck stayed upright.

As soon as I stepped between the trees I felt the cold again, the frozen breath of winter, awoken. I felt my teeth chatter, knees buckle. It wasn't natural, this cold. The air stung my face and I recoiled, pressing my jacket sleeve against it. I could feel tiny tears in the corner of my eyes, though they froze as soon as they appeared.

I took shaky steps forward, wild eyes darting every time I heard a sound. The wind howled between the branches and the trees, quiet at first and then louder as I walked. The trees moaned and shifted beneath the winter winds, a mournful cacophony of nature.

I froze mid-step, my eyes wide and my body stiff. In between the howling wind and creaking trees, I heard someone say my name.

Not in the way a concerned parent calls out to you, or the way an annoying sibling tries to get your attention. No, there was no love in this familiar word. The voice I heard was creaking and slow, one I had never heard before nor wish to hear again. It wasn't a call but a whisper, one that had somehow reached me despite the eerie sounds of nature.

I heard it again, closer. Either from the cold or from fear, I was frozen in place. Only my eyes would move where I would tell them to; my body was frozen like the landscape itself.

Again, the whisper grew in my ears. I felt my already panicked breathing quicken.

My name, again. Whispered from behind me, getting closer. The sounds of my name were grotesquely stretched by the creaking voice, and I heard the hints of malice.

And then the woods were silent. No wind, no creaking trees. No spectral voice among the still snow.

Something grabbed my shoulder.

I felt my terror rise through my throat in a hoarse, guttural scream. The Something grasped me tightly and pain shot through my shoulder.

I darted my eyes down towards my shoulder. Fingers did not hold me. Long, grey appendages that bent at odd angles had pierced through my jacket. They looked like the barren and dead branches of the oak trees above me.

The Something whispered my name again, death in its voice.

I screamed again, tearing my shoulder away. Despite the cold I ran, with God as my witness, I ran. I ran through the snow banks, over fallen trees and branches, in between patches of ice and bare earth.

My steps were awkward from the height of the snow. I held my camera with both hands so as not to drop it, though without the use of my arms to balance myself I nearly tripped multiple times.

The sound of the winter winds picked up again with a furious roar, tearing through the trees behind me. I felt the torrent of wind press against my back, and I knew the Something was chasing me.

Again, I felt the ice cold branch-like fingers touch me, brushing against the base of my neck. I could feel the cold tears against my cheeks freeze as I threw my camera to the ground, using my arms to help balance myself. I ran faster as the Something called out to me.

My house came into view through the trees.

"Help!" I had screamed. "Help! Help me!"

Help, the Something whispered behind me with its ghoulish, creaking voice. Help. Help me.

I screamed in terror, exhaustion overcoming my lungs. I could feel the burning heat in my legs beg me to stop, to take a breather. But the edge of the forest came into sight and, with an insane surge of fear driven energy, I threw myself out of the forest and into my house's snowy backyard.

My parents, God bless them, were running from the house before I had even stood up. My flannel-pajama wearing mother had frantically thrown on her winter boots. My father ran through the snow barefoot, wearing only a robe.

"Help!" I screamed again, my voice hysteric. "There's something in the woods!"

My parents caught me, held me as I screamed over and over. They tried to console me, to reassure me that everything was okay. And yet still, I shouted. *Help. Help. Help me!*

A few hours later, I was enveloped in a warm blanket with an untouched mug of steaming hot chocolate on the coffee table before me. My parents tried to calm me; they themselves were calmer, now, but still deeply concerned for their terrified child. They told me that the woods were big and scary for a little one, and that it was okay to be afraid. When I told them of the whispered words, of the branch-fingers on my shoulder, they told me that I had imagined it: the whispers were just the sound of wind across the snow, the holes in my jacket from a low-hanging branch.

My parents, truly the warmest, most logical people in the world, managed to calm me down. I started to believe that, just maybe, my experience in the woods had been the work of an overactive imagination. My sisters and brother even began teasing me for it, saying that the Something would come and take me away.

And yet, despite my family's reassurance, I could not shake the feeling that they were wrong. Sometimes, when I looked out at the woods from my warm bedroom's window, I would feel the hair stand up as it had on that day. If I looked long enough, no matter how many blankets I had on, I would start to feel the creeping cold that had frozen me to my bones on that day.

It took me thirty years and a lot of therapy to get over those memories. I was never comfortable going out in winter by myself again. As I grew older, I left my northern home to move south for school and never looked back. Nowadays I make my living as a nature photographer for a national magazine, specialized in old-school film techniques – though I refuse to work anywhere that has snow during the winter season.

A few days ago, I got a call from my aging mother. My father had recently passed and she was selling our family house. My sisters, brother, and I went up to visit and help her pack away our childhood memories.

From my mother's front porch I looked out at the woods, green and warm beneath the summer sun. Whether it was the time away or the lack of frozen death, I no longer feared this place. With my brother as backup, I went down to face my childhood fears.

We walked for a while, reminiscing on our youth. Pointed out the areas where we made our snow angels and our forts, as well as the beach where we would swim during the summer. Filled with warmth, we were headed back towards the house when I saw a glint of metal partially buried beside a tree.

My old camera.

Despite the fear I had felt that day, I remembered that perfect shot. The blues and the whites and the oranges. The last normal day of my youth. I picked the camera up, joking with my brother. I doubted the photo would look great after all of this time, but I am something of a wizard when it comes to developing film.

I returned down south, where I am writing this now. I developed the photo about three hours ago. To my surprise, it had only partial damage to it, blotching out the sun but leaving much of the shot intact. Reminiscing, I told myself that my parents had been right after all. Beneath the red light of the dark room I had happily taken the sights in, reminding myself of the days of the young winter lover, marvelling at the river, the snow, the trees...

And that's when I saw it.

Standing among the birch trees, hidden just behind, I saw a figure staring back at me. It was tall and incredibly thin, with a body that was the same waxy-white as the trees that surrounded it. Its arms and legs were twice as long as its body, branch-thin and grey as death. At the end of its limbs were the branch-like fingers that had torn into my jacket thirty years ago, thin and long and sharp.

Atop its giant, emaciated body, the Something's featureless, porcelain-white face stared back at me, as if through the photograph itself. Its eyes were black and wide and empty, its mouth a broken, jagged crack in the mask-like face.

I fell to the floor within my darkroom, the horrible memories flooding back. I screamed, just as I had that day. I screamed and screamed and screamed until I could only whimper. I felt the cold, the hair on my neck, the horrible grasp of the Something on my shoulder.

And now I write this, before it's too late. My family won't believe me, my friends will think I'm insane.

But I need to share this story now. I don't think I have much time left.

Because, even though it's thirty degrees Celsius where I live, snow just began to fall outside my window.

NEW LIFE
Meredith Field
Medium: Watercolor
Dimensions: 5x7

THE GLASS.

DS Maolalai

this pink skin
circles a scar
which came to my hand
by means of a wineglass
washed too hard
and cracked.

which came to my sink
from a second hand shop,
which came to them
by someone not knowing what to do
with the things left over
in grandmother's house,
and came to her

by means of a salesman,
by means of a craftsman,
by means of rocks, rocks
ground up by water
by means of the sea
until they were sand

which was boiled in pots
until it was glass

which was carefully blown
until it was shaped
which was shipped
via the salesman
the grandmother
to the second hand shop
over 80 years
until one got to me

and I broke it
washing
too hard
and it went in the trash
to go
god knows where
after the dumps
are dug up

by irradiated robots
or aliens
curious as to human life
and meanwhile

the only testament
to the sandrakers
or the glassblowers
skill in creation
or the salesman's skill
in closing a deal
will be this little
pink line on my finger

destined
to slough off
like chocolate
on a tongue
when I'm lowered to the ground
in a few years

and my stuff
off to charity,

leaving bones
and some dirt
with fewer scars
than fingers.

THE MUSIC OF HOOFBEATS AND HEARTS

Lennart Lundh

I hope you remember when we were
younger, the golden horse on the carousel,
you seated behind me warm against my back
with your arms around my waist, the
calliope sound and our hearts, how the
horse came to life and galloped across the
midway, carrying us so far away as it sang
most beautifully to reassure us we were
right in the moment and for each other.
Wherever you are, I hope you remember
we had music in our life for a while.

WISHES

Lauro Palomba

"I'd like my dead friends
back, all of them
and I want us to be
thirty years younger"

carping it wasn't
couldn't have been
he'd signed over
his objections, already
seven weeks beyond
the best before date
for joining them

echoed in the hospice
parking lot, we doubted
we'd ever heard anything
less unreasonable

he loved horses
the week before
we'd trailered one
reversed onto the hospice
patio for him to touch

SANCTUARIES

Christopher Watkins

Let me speak not of goodness,
or of how one should live.
Instead, let me speak
of an ordinary white oak
with its green, caterpillar-legged leaves
and its thick, quick-branching trunk;
bottom limbs that curve down
to almost touch the ground,
and a radius that arches
from there to the topmost branch
in a rounded, family dome.

And let me speak
not of good things dying,
but of leaves turning red—
not the red of lost blood,
the red of a newborn child's palm.
Let me acknowledge the silent look
of an empty bough
waiting for snow to whisper
on the surface of its near-black bark.
Yet let me speak also of hope.
For there is hope for a tree,
if it is cut down,
that it will sprout again.

Let me speak not of goodness,
but only of trees,
so that everything may become clear
and we may begin to understand
ourselves.

UNTITLED
Erica Shimmel
Medium: Photo

HOW TO FIND AN AGATE

W. Joseph Lutz

With special thanks to the
Gitche Gumee Landing
gift shop

First you go out as the evening begins
with the piles of stones lying on the beach
between you and the setting sun.
Look for the ones that sparkle, not just shine.
All of them shine while they are wet,
then as they dry, slowly to reveal
an unremarkable pebble of shale.
But look for the sparkle, that glint of glory
that designates an authentic treasure.
Find it. Capture it.
Hold it close to your heart.

THE PERSEIDS

Steven Dale Davison

On the mountain pond the stars
step out onto obsidian
smooth, and a dark as deep
as star beams are lean.

The dome above revolves,
the last indigo fading
into background black
for the wheeling constellations.

As lightquiet counterpoint
to bullfrog songs, the moon
rises. A loon cries. The restless
winds lay down their wings.

Through the night we doze,
awaken, snug deeper in our bag,
watch the soundless Perseids streak
in extra terra visitation.

EARTH-BOUND

Louisa Howerow

if I had known
as a child

my foot was forged
in a belly of a star

hand   ear   eye   the whole
of me   stardust

I would have
escaped the nightly
clutch of blankets
to my chest

crushed the infinite
dark

I would have
pulled back curtains

opened windows
to the night's spark

as joy as firefly
reached out and up

a child to the stars--
this is you this is me

THE SUN AND THE BEAR

Gregor Southard

The bear,
eyes still closed,
emerged from his rocky bedroom.
The late winter cold
of his sleeping spot
lingered on the hair covering
his face, flesh, and skin.

The bear,
he shrugged
his shoulders vigorously
before the sun emerged,
kicking off said coolness.
He looked up
at the source of warmth,
almost appearing to smile.

The sun,
he said, "I missed you."
The bear,
he replied, "I was very tired."

The sun,
he said, "it was like we

were made for each other."
The bear,
he offered, "I had a dream
that we, in fact, were."

CRAVING 1
Fariel Shafee
Medium: Watercolor pencils on paper
Dimensions: 12x18 inches

PAPER CHILD

Joseph Crossley

I had sketched my son to the best of my ability. His lines blurred around his right shoulder, and there was a place on his lower lip where I had smudged the pencil with my finger. His faults were my faults.

I met him today when I came home from work. I had worked two all-day shifts over the weekend at the restaurant and was coming home, walking east with the rising sun. I crossed the road, walking past the tall oak tree that grew outside my building. Inside, I headed for the stairs, returning the greetings of my superintendent, Mr. Prager, with a curt nod. His morning check on his property done, he was on his way to breakfast at a kosher food cart. The time was nine o'clock.

I was ready to fall asleep in my doorway when I found him, a man made of paper, sitting on my sofa. He was formed of rolled sheets, bound by a force unseen. He was blank on his rear side, his features drawn on his front.

I rubbed my eyes, hoping this thing was a product of my faulty vision. He remained.

The paper man was moving. His hands, his lips, his eyes, they were articulate. Clumsy, but they worked.

He turned to me and said, as far as he knew, he was my son. He was reading *My Big Family*, one of a few children's books belonging to my sister. She was here with her daughter last week and she left them behind.

I'm your son, he said, and you're my dad. He pointed to the letters on the page one by one. My D-A-D.

Drawing was my hobby. It suppressed memories of long shifts and bad dates and bills paid past due.

I was able to draw most of a person, except for the face. I was terrible with faces, always worrying about the bridge of the nose and squashing the mouth and the eyes.

Three nights ago, I decided I'd have one more go at a face. Pressing just right on the paper with my pencil, letting my hand relax and go with the lines as they came to me, I was there an hour at the desk in the corner of my flat, a lamp held up by tape casting a weak glow overhead. Finished, I dropped the pencil and pushed back my chair, taking in my creation.

I slept well after completing my work, and hated it by morning. I had dreamt of something better, more alive and beautiful and true. I threw the drawing in my wastepaper basket. He didn't like that.

"It was cold in there," he said. "Cold and hard."

"How can you talk?" I said.

"I learnt the words from this."

He handed me the copy of *My Big Family*. Flipping through it, I noticed there was a section within specifically for parents, which made use of a larger vocabulary than the rest of the book.

"But how do you produce sounds?" I said.

"I don't know. How do you produce sounds?"

I admitted I was unsure, muttering a line about vocal chords I remembered from ninth grade science class.

"You're much bigger than I drew you."

"You were a baby, weren't you?" he said, showing me a picture of an infant on the cover of my sister's book.

"I was, years ago."

"You grew. So did I."

The paper man said he assembled his body from my old sketches. I recognised a drawing of a hand I had attempted. He'd taken the sketches from the wastepaper basket and fastened a body. To complete his peculiar process of evolution, he had climbed out, grown, found the book and read.

He had been waiting. For his "dad," he said, once he knew the word. He had waited for his dad to come home.

Saying nothing, I studied him. Every part of him was careful, innocent and sweet. I wanted to touch him, and I put out my hand. He grasped my fingers in a newborn's way, reassuring himself I was there. There was no warmth in his hand. There was no warmth in the room. Mr. Prager didn't care to fix the heating.

I had an urge to reject him, or to believe I really had fallen asleep in the doorway, and this was a lucid dream. I felt he was wrong, so offensive that the only sound course of action was to put distance between us both and let us never be close.

He *was* a child. If I commanded him, he might leave my home forever. Or, what if *I* left, promising to soon return, and never making good on my word?

But I let him stay, and made no promises I couldn't keep. It was nice to have company, and he seemed a decent kid.

"Do you have a name?" I said.

"Not yet. I've seen a lot of names and they were all wrong."

He showed me the legal details printed on the inside cover of *My Big Family*.

"These names are strange," he said. "I don't want to be called 'Penguin' or 'Viking.'"

"Then we can give you a normal name."

"Do you have a normal name?"

"Yes. I'm Nick."

I pointed to the name of the book's author.

"Here we go," I said, "his name's Robert. How does that sound?"

"Robert."

"Yeah, you're Robert. I'm your dad, so I'll call you Rob."

"We're Rob and Nick."

"That's us. That's you and me."

* * *

We were together in my apartment for three weeks. It was us, the shouting neighbours, the freezing draught, and the smell of falafel in the mornings. I was stagnating. Rob was puzzled. We went on, despite it all.

Rob started to test "you and me," and it proved to be a bond that weathered fast. It was his questioning that did it — his endless stream of questioning.

"Where am I, Nick?"

"My living room."

"And Nick, what's outside the living room?'

I pointed to the sleeping bag on the floor. "Over there's my bedroom." I pointed to a door. "Bathroom's through there." Then to the hall. "That's the way to the front door."

"And Nick?"

"What?"

"Nick, what's outside the front door?"

He wanted to learn. Everything he encountered he asked me, at once, what it was. Being an idiot, I always told him.

I said, "That's a tree. It grows tall and it has green leaves at the top."

Or, "A rock. Rocks are grey, see here," I said, pointing to the area of wallpaper darkened by water damage, "that colour. And rocks are tough. You know, hard."

Or, "No, most children don't come from wastepaper baskets."

I had my own questions — what his first memory was, how he came alive, if there were other paper people elsewhere – and I never asked any of them. I didn't want to encourage him. The book my sister left told me to be a model parent. Act as you want them to act, it said. They will follow you.

I was trying to draw, and Rob kept pestering me.

"Nick?"

I outlined the chin on the face of my new drawing. It was to be another face. In every way it would be better than my last attempt.

"Nick?"

"What do you want?" I said.

"Why aren't you talking?"

"I'm in the middle of drawing."

"Can you help me with something?"

"Depends what it is."

"I'm trying to read this book, but I can't make out the pictures."

He had finished with *My Big Family* and was reading its sequel, *My Big Farm*.

"That book doesn't have any pictures in it," I said.

"Yes, it does," said Rob, "the words are always mentioning the pictures the characters can see, but I can't see any of them in my head."

He meant to say he was unable to comprehend the imagery. I repeated to him what he was attempting to express, and he rephrased his question. He said he'd never seen the things mentioned in the book, these "sheep," "cows," and "pigs," When he read the book, he saw only the words, without any meaning. There was no charm for him, beyond the aesthetic pleasures of the ink.

"Can't you read without seeing them?" I said.

"I can, but it's hard."

"Put up with it."

"You're being rude to me. You weren't being rude before."

"I have every right, and every reason to be rude. You're disturbing me."

"Sorry, Nick."

"Give me quiet, okay?"

"Okay."

"Good boy. And if you don't talk for a *really* long time, I'll help you with the pictures."

That silenced him. Rob did as I asked for a few hours and let me finish my drawing. In the end, of course, I was unhappy with it. The left side of the face didn't match the right, and the nose started too far below the eyes.

I crumpled the drawing into a ball. I never redid a drawing. My mistakes were behind me, and fixing them was tedious.

Halfway to dropping the ball of paper in the wastepaper basket, I thought better of it. I didn't want another child. Best leave this latest error sitting here. It was in my sight, but not alive. The creases and folds hid the problems.

In my head, I pictured a better drawing on the paper, to which I had no obligation to return.

"Nick?"

"Can't you give me even five minutes of silence?"

"You've had hours."

"Don't you speak to me that way. You're never to speak to me that way."

You idiot, I thought. They will follow. Act as you want them to act.

"I'm sorry," said Rob.

"I'm sorry as well. Go on, ask the question."

I flattened a blank sheet of paper and set to work on a fresh project. Not a human face. A dog. I needed diversity in my work. Enough with humans, I thought, I draw dogs now.

"Nick, what do you do? As a job, I mean."

"I bus tables."

Rob was nonplussed.

"I *clean* tables. In a restaurant a couple blocks from here."

"Can I visit?"

"Absolutely not."

How does one draw a dog's face? I started with the nose.

"Why can't I go to the restaurant? I really want to."

"One," I said, "You can't walk. Two, people aren't used to you. And three, it's boring. You wouldn't like it."

"I bet I would like it. Tell me what you do."

"I did that already."

"Tell me more."

"Maybe later. Go finish your book."

"I want to hear about the restaurant."

"I said finish your book. And be quiet."

I didn't appreciate his curiosity. My life was my own. It was enough to experience what I did, he had no business forcing me to explain it to him.

I decided I had no use for Rob in my life. He had incredible potential, but whatever brilliant, complete person he might become would have to remain a dream.

He was the same as the drawing on my desk. Instead of working to improve him, I imagined him as better than he was. It was a pleasant thought. A shame it would never come true. All I needed now was a way to be rid of him.

One day I heard my solution. It was a low and distant rumble.

I had shut my curtains to stop Rob finding things outside to talk about. Pulling them apart and looking at the sky, I saw what I needed. Grey clouds, gathering in the distance. Coming our way. Act as you want them to act. They will follow you.

It was nine o'clock. Mr. Prager was out for breakfast, my neighbours out at work. We were alone.

In the beginning, Rob was a fresh, enthralling project. Then he became real and human, a problem I didn't have the time to concern myself with.

"You want to see the pictures?" I said.

"Oh, I do."

"I don't know how to find sheep, cows, or pigs. But I promise there's a tree."

He was delighted. Outside, there was thunder sounding two seconds after lightning flashed. It was coming closer.

I picked up Rob in my arms. He was light, and I discovered he was hollow. Hauling him over my shoulder, I carried him into the hallway. I silenced his questions, reminding him he may frighten people. He wasn't fit for public display. We didn't want to frighten people, now did we? No, said Rob, no we didn't.

Beyond my front door, the whole building was clouded in the stifled humidity that precedes a storm. Feeling the stiff carpet below my feet, myself equally tense, I got us both to the elevator and pushed the button for the first floor. We crawled downwards at a painful speed. At last, the bell rang, and the doors opened. I peered into the lobby; no sign of Mr. Prager. The weather couldn't contain that man's appetite. I hurried to the front door.

Plastic single-pane windows fronted the concrete walls of the lobby. The whole room stank of damp and rubber, and above us I heard a woman screaming at her child. Beyond the plastic windows there was grass, and standing among the grass was the tall oak tree, shaking in the wind.

"That, Rob, is a tree," I said.

real tree."

"That's right. Come on, let's look for a rock."

"Nick, wait."

I answered him in my softest voice.

"What's the matter?" I said.

"I want to walk. Without help."

"You can't walk."

"I've never tried. That doesn't mean I can't do it."

I allowed him this last pleasure.

"Fine. You want to walk, you can walk," I said.

I let Rob down to the ground and held him under his arms, keeping him up, his legs dangling and feet resting on the floor. I stepped away, and released him from my grasp. I helped open the front door for him. My son stood and took his first step, me holding only the tips of his fingers.

"Hurry up, come on," I said.

The rubber smell was burning my nostrils. He was almost at the door.

"You can do it, one more big step."

He looked exhausted, ready to collapse.

"I can't do it," said Rob.

"You can. One more big step, there we go."

One more step. One more, and he made it. He was outside. Rob met the world, and the world met Rob.

The first drops of rain fell. I shut the door behind him. He looked at his arm where the rain hit him and watched, confused, as the water sunk into his skin.

"Nick?"

"Yeah?"

"What's happening to me?"

"Well, it's raining. You're getting wet. Don't they explain what rain is in your books?"

"They do, but they didn't mention *this.*"

He pulled at a strand of his skin that was breaking up. It rained heavier and faster, and in the distance I heard more thunder.

"Nick?"

"Yeah, Rob?"

"I'm scared. I don't know what's happening. Oh, I want it to stop, please make it stop."

His right arm started to break off. The paper around his shoulder wasn't strong enough to carry the weight. Rob screamed, stumbled and fell to the floor, and as he landed he crashed to the ground and lost the arm.

"It's okay," I said.

"I want to go back in," said Rob. "I want to go back to the apartment."

"I know."

"Please take me back to the apartment. Please, Nick."

"It's okay."

Rob begged me to help. The sounds of his screaming were drowned amidst the thunder. I closed my eyes. When I looked again, he was staring at me, still hoping I would save him.

Next to go were his legs. The rain tore them both apart at the knee, then the hip. We were on the path outside my building that cuts through the grass. The path slanted in such a way that, as each part of Rob fell off him, the resulting mass of wet paper fell and washed off to either side of me.

All that was left of him on the path was his head and his torso. His torso was caved in.

"Nick?"

CRAVING 3
Fariel Shafee
Medium: Watercolor and watercolor pencils on paper
Dimensions: 18x12 inches

EDITORS' CHOICE

THE DREAMER FINDS A BLUE FLOWER

Stephen Linsteadt

Medium: Oil on canvas

Dimensions: 72x86 inches

WOMAN ENOUGH

jd Hegarty

i want to be all of the things I am / all at once until i die
i'm a baby who has been alive for twenty six years.
Joshua Jennifer Espinoza

Today, again, I cut myself shaving.
They don't make razors sharp

enough to pare down this face
until the mirror looks like me—

lasers are cost prohibitive—
settle for red turned pink as it

spills down the drain.
I've been dieting again,

trying to shrink already before
I have a specialist to prescribe

what I need to grow into myself:
estrogen can cause

weight gain and I'm already
extra-large in newfound clothing.

And I don't want to be a big-boned
girl, not because there's

anything wrong with extra-large,
but I don't need that kind of attention.

I get it already, like the first time
I wore a skirt outside my own home

and a stranger took issue with
my existence, not for who I was, but how

I let others say he and him. Like
I need to fight every battle every moment

or I am not woman enough or I am not trans
enough for her eyes, for her comfort,

like I don't switch codes easy as breathing,
like I don't pack my womanhood away

each morning, suit up for strangers to call me sir,
sit in an office where no one knows who I am

outside of it, where I tell no one who I am
who could take anything away from me

because I need a paycheck more than I need
to be seen, at least today. I already

risked my father's love and I don't think
I can win like that again, where all he wanted to know

is *so if you're my daughter, does that make you*
a lesbian? when I was so sure he would be all

about how *well, you'll always be my son* and
I love you no matter what and when I was wrong

about him, the place in me that used to know
how to cry started to tremble again. As a child

I thought I was an alien, an extra-terrestrial
who couldn't understand the other kids

and cried when no one looked because I
didn't understand how to be a person

and eventually I stopped crying but at twenty-six
still struggle with how to be a person. I say

a name and it feels like a question. I say another
and it feels like a lie. I introduce myself to strangers

under any collection of signifiers, but nothing
feels like the home I'm not ready to build. The

distance between where I am and where I
need to be. My every step forward staggered by

metaphysical doubt even when I know who I am, always.

And isn't it so terrible that we have to exist

embodied? Or that we are these bodies and
also are not these bodies? On some days, I

feel as transparent as a pane of glass
but on most, I draw the blinds. Ignore my

neighbors. Ignore texts from my mother.
Forgetting to check in with my friends,

like I'm the only one with issues. But I don't
have the energy and I'm sorry, but I just

don't have it in me today to do much
besides pet my cats who don't care who

I am as long as they get fed twice a day.
The simplicity of animals: a friend I hadn't told once

said her dog doesn't usually like men. Another friend
before I even knew, said her cat loves boys. And both

loved on me without suspicion and isn't that
really all that anyone wants? Isn't that enough?

PERHAPS

DS Maolalai

in ireland
it's 11pm. in toronto
6, and 3 of my
ex-girlfriends
just out of work.
perhaps, anyway. we're not really
in touch. perhaps
one is working nights now,
or maybe
doesn't work at all -
she's in the park
looking at bluebirds
or drinking a glass of water.

it's just the end of may;
if I remember right
things get hot there
this time of year. perhaps
she's trying on a new hat right now,
or on a date
or an organised night out
in her last year of college.

spirits

within spirits move. memory;
yells in a cave
bouncing quietly. it's hot on spadina,
burning squirrels black. the sun
a dusky red
between two buildings. and clean ground
cuts in two
and separates - goes sideways - cora, melissa
and cheryl (not knowing each other
at all) perhaps sharing
the same streetcar
as it rises
like a lizard
from the ground.

UNTITLED

XIAOLI NEWELL

UNINHABITED

Ellie Roscher

"I just saw the mouse again," Dan reported, entering our bedroom wearing only his towel. He took a longer look at me, and his annoyance fell away. With a mischievous expression, he approached me from behind and cupped each breast lovingly in his hands. "Your breasts look gigantic."

I pondered my reflection in the mirror. "They do," I agreed. "Maybe I'm pregnant," I added playfully before walking away.

Once I said it, the possibility took up space. The sound bite kept repeating in my mind. In the shower, on the Downtown A train, typing on my work computer, my womb resonated with the hypothesis each time. *Maybe* I am. I spent the morning smiling at my little secret. *Maybe.* Each trip to the bathroom confirmed what I was beginning to believe was true. No blood. A coy *maybe* evolved to a hopeful one. Dabbling became desire.

On my way home from work I swung into Duane Reade on 125th Street and Amsterdam and purchased a two-pack pregnancy test. As the man rang up the singular purchase, there was no trace of embarrassment or conflict in my demeanor. I wanted to be pregnant. I was eager to become a mother. I was a prepared student this time, eager to pass the test.

On my way to the bathroom I sped by Dan, who was preoccupied with scoring a loaf of bread. I knew I was supposed to wait for morning, but the urgency to name my new reality blurred my better judgement. I was nervous and awkward. I fumbled. I peed crooked. The test was inconclusive. I spent the night irrationally withdrawn.

Morning brought renewed wonder and butterflies in my stomach. I urinated with calm precision. Minutes later, waves of joy lapped over me, one after another. I gasped and then giggled. A perfect, undeniable, blue cross. Something alive had taken root in my body. I was full of potential.

Dan was elated. He researched doctors in Harlem. I started taking pre-natal vitamins. We meandered up Riverside Drive and talked about when we should share the news and imagined how people would react. We cheered on our little bundle of cells. I kept the pregnancy test on the sink, smiling at it multiple times a day, needing a mirror held up to my truth. Dan suggested taking a picture of it so we could throw it away, but played with the aperture on the camera long enough to validate my excitement, pulling the cross into focus against the vanity.

My fashionable girlfriend took me to Athleta to help create a maternity wardrobe. I was reluctant to make such temporary investments, so she steered me to items that shrink and expand with me. I bought two stretchy shirts, as well as a pair of loose, lightweight black pants with a wide and forgiving elastic waistband. They were delectable. I named them my butter pants and began wearing them regularly. I braced myself to gain weight.

Dan and I started a list of names. I eliminated alcohol and coffee, deli meat and shellfish and then, when nausea set in, all food except saltines and broth. Busy preparing a home, my body collapsed onto the couch after each workday. Each nap felt nonnegotiable. Sleep felt like mercy. I was repulsed by Dan's smell and had to cover my nose with a blanket when we sat on the couch together. When I entered our apartment after work each day, I was overwhelmed by the smell of the food Dan had eaten hours before. Days were long and hard. I felt lucky. We uploaded an app on my phone that updated us on the baby's progress. Dan talked to my belly according to its multiplying size. *Hello, my little lentil. Good morning, my lovely cashew. I'm your dad.* I was unrelentingly constipated. My body had been taken over. I tried to approach my misery with curiosity. I tried to get out of the way.

Then one morning, sitting on the toilet, I recoiled at what I was holding. Contrasting the bright white nest of toilet paper in my hand was an amorphous glob of tissue, midnight blue streaked with shiny crimson.

"Shit."

"What?" Dan called from the kitchen, alarmed.

"I'm bleeding," was all I said, but already it felt more conclusive than that.

The bleeding continued and the cramping began, both much more intense than my monthly menstruation. It felt like my uterus was being kneaded. The blood and tissue loss was steady. I shook with the intensity of not wanting what was happening to be happening.

Dan, desperate for something to do, called the doctor's office. I wilted on the couch and curled into the pain, breathing deeply. The nurse would not talk to him. I was the patient. He handed me the phone.

"Tell me what's happening," a woman said.

"I'm bleeding heavily and cramping. Should I come in?"

"No, there is nothing we can do. It sounds like you are miscarrying. I will have a nurse call you tomorrow."

"Okay," I said. "Thank you."

My body moved almost involuntarily to maintain my schedule. I took the subway to Columbus Circle to meet with my thesis advisor, stopping by Duane Reade for heavy duty pads on the way. I grabbed a bag of gummy bears at the counter, a pathetic attempt at comfort. When my advisor asked if I'd been crying, I blamed it on the beauty of the Paul Monette essay I was reading. I wrote down what she said so I could reference it later. I was hearing but not listening. My body was seeping. We spoke of her work, her love life, my writing, my thesis, and my impending graduation. There was so much to feel so little about.

That evening, I sat down on the couch, took a deep breath and picked up the phone to call my mom. After floating from above in denial all day, I dropped back into my body. I tucked my knees into my stomach and held them there. I heard my voice say, "I am losing the baby." I started sobbing huge, lurching sobs. Saying it aloud felt like confessing. Saying it aloud made it real. True.

"Oh honey, oh, I'm so sorry," she said. "I wish this wasn't happening. I wish I could take this away from you. I wish I could be there to hold you. I remember."

She struggled to conceive. The doctors told her she could not have children and then, after a stillborn baby, she had five healthy kids. I was supposed to feel hope from her story. Instead I felt depleted and hollow. She felt far away. I wandered into bed and closed my swollen eyes.

I went to work the next day, not quite knowing what else to do. The cloud surrounding me was laced with shame. With a whispering voice, shaky through tears, I told my boss what was happening. She hugged me, then launched into her story. She had seven miscarriages before flying to Russia to adopt three children with special needs. I could barely hear her, the sound of my own love lost consuming my ears. Midday, I moved to the hallway to take a call from a nurse. "I'm bleeding a lot. It's like my period but heavier, thicker, more painful. It has been a full day now," I told her.

She scheduled an appointment at a lab down the street from my apartment to have blood drawn to check hormone levels and confirm the miscarriage. Dozens of strangers walked past while I was on the phone. How could no one tell that my chest was exposed to the wind? How could they not stare in horror at my body being evacuated?

That night I had a primal urge to amble the streets of Manhattan. I imagined finding a loose square of sidewalk, ripping at it until my fingernails were raw, until I came in contact with dirt. My body wanted to squat and bleed into the earth directly. Instead, I stayed inside, leaving the couch only to change my pad every few hours.

Dan dealt with his disembodied loss by fixating on catching the mice in our apartment. He pulled the stove out and deep cleaned the floor. He set new traps. He researched best practices and explored the apartment for clues.

I fixated on my blood, which was all I had left. One morning in the shower, a particularly large clump of tissue got stopped in our hair catcher. I bent down, picked it up, and rolled it around between my fingertips, searching for signs of life. I wanted to see a baby. I wanted proof. I put the clot in the toilet but could not bring myself to flush it down.

It took several phone calls and an hour on hold to have my lab results confirm what I already knew.

"Hi. My name is Ellie Roscher. I'm calling back about my hormone levels from lab work. To confirm a miscarriage."

"Yes, you miscarried," was all the man said.

"Okay, thank you."

Something became nothing. I called my siblings and a few friends and told them that I was pregnant and now I am not. *This is totally normal. One in four women miscarry. Just keep trying.* There is such little vocabulary for this loss. It is grieving an idea, slowly reeling back in the carpet that had already unrolled ahead of you, filled with potential moments of little hands and innocent laughter. It's looking at a space created in the world and wondering how it would ever be filled. It's looking at every pregnant belly and every baby through the lens of loss, wondering what could have been. It's longing for something unseen, untouched.

The next day, I called the clinic one last time to cancel my next baby wellness checkup.

"Do you need to reschedule?" a woman asked.

"No, I miscarried," I said.

"I'm sorry," she said. It was the first compassionate word I heard from that office.

I reintroduced coffee and alcohol, deli meat and shellfish. I went to work. I went to class. I worked on my thesis. I watched a beautiful little girl twirling circles on the subway platform to the guitar music of a street performer. I watched her parents watch her. Dan watched me watch them. I watched until I had to turn away. Our best friends called to announce that they were pregnant, due a week before ours would have been. Dan and I passed the phone back and forth, sharing our excitement and encouragement with them. Once we hung up, Dan cried for the first time. He told me he could feel the loss. The absence resided in the possibility of raising our children together. He had yet to catch a mouse.

Just three months after the miscarriage, with the pain still raw and consuming, I got pregnant again. Instead of joy I felt exhaustion and dread. It felt like betrayal. I hated my caution, my skepticism, my preparation for an inevitable death. It was too soon. The grief was too thick, too heavy. I was still getting to know the child I would never meet. I eliminated coffee and alcohol, deli meat and shellfish again. I switched to a new clinic. When I told people my mouth smiled, but my eyes did not. Nausea, bloating and constipation set in and took hold. I curled in on my enlarged breasts, guarded.

Dan was timidly happy. We paced ourselves. I turned in my thesis and took my last classes. I ate stacks of saltines at my work desk. My graduation ceremony was outside, and the smell of grass made me sick. I focused on not puking while Vera Wang gave a lovely speech. Dan decided we needed a change in scenery and found cheap tickets to Puerto Rico for a long weekend.

The cobblestone streets of Old San Juan smelled of fermenting fruit. Vibrant pink hibiscus crawled up blue and yellow walls. We wandered through the heat. My body was either asleep or longing to be so. I watched Dan sip rum. The clouds, full of rain, held their breath. The mountains whispered ancient hymns. I did not know what language to speak. I did not belong in such a beautiful place.

The musty hotel we shared with artists and shamans was cluttered with chipped busts, spider plants and nymphs spitting water. One night we climbed to the rooftop patio and sat. The wind off the Atlantic caught my breath and something inside me came unstuck. Grief spilled. *I do not want this baby.* I admitted silently to myself. *I want the dead one.*

The tangled ball of yarn in my chest took a slow, full breath. I sat there for a long time, rooted, watching a large ship leave the bay.

In the heat of late summer, I spent the morning packing for a short term research trip to Kenya and a permanent move to Minnesota. I stayed pregnant. My feelings remained muted and conflicted, no trace of recapturing the joy of the first pregnancy. Yet each new day brought hints of curiosity and glimpses of hope. *Maybe.*

I left boxes and suitcases open, kissed Dan goodbye, and headed to my second baby wellness check-up. The nurse informed me that I had lost weight, but my vitals were strong. The doctor started the ultrasound. As the image came into focus, her demeanor changed.

"Oh. Oh, no. Oh, I'm sorry. The baby stopped developing four weeks ago. There's no heartbeat anymore." I watched her reach down, grab the automatic image print out, and throw it in the trash. "We should get it out as soon as we can so it doesn't cause an infection. Let me go check my schedule."

She hurried out of the room, leaving me alone, undone. Ravaged and weary. A nurse came in to turn over the room, surprised to see me. Desperate to escape the pain welling up inside of me, I offered to go to the waiting room. Maybe if I kept moving it wouldn't be true. Maybe if I put her needs before my own, mine would disappear. I soon regretted my choice. I sat among two women bursting with life. Expansive and happy. One was rubbing her belly. The other was holding the hand of a man next to her.

The nurse approached. "Are you free tomorrow?"

I was. We set up a procedure time and I left.

I decided to keep a date with my friend who lived in Chelsea. I could feel the shame looming and the sadness breathing but coped through disconnecting. We sat in her garden sipping tea. I didn't tell her about my day. She didn't know I was pregnant or not pregnant, a difference that now felt like a treacherous chasm. Whiplash. A distinction that altered reality and shifted identity more intensely than any other I had known. In her gaze, I was simply the person she knew me to be- a friend, graduate student and writer. For an hour or two, I could pretend. It was a kind, welcome respite from an existential spiral.

"Hi," Dan called from his home office, unassuming, when I got home. I let him finish what he was doing, prolonging speaking. Eventually he came in and joined me on the couch. "How was your appointment?"

Finally, I started to cry. "The baby stopped growing. I'm going in tomorrow to get it removed." I knew something was happening to him and to us, but I could not get out from under the thing that was happening to me. The aloneness startled me. *Was it because I didn't let myself attach? Was I not a suitable environment for life to take hold? Why wouldn't my body let the baby go?*

Twice the role of being a mother presented itself. Twice the existence of a baby made itself known. A different life unfolded in front of me now, filled with bitterness and void. I saw myself sidelined by a heavy vacuousness. What if this is my story?

I sent a group text to my family and a group email to my friends. The responses felt anemic and added to the isolating shame and despair. *God has a plan. This will work out. The pain will go away once you have a baby.* Dan brought me white wine and M&Ms. I tried to offer whatever was inside of me affection, to sense it before it was taken away, but it remained an elusive idea.

"The mouse," I whispered to Dan as I watched it scamper across the kitchen floor.

The next morning I opted for comfort, pulling my black butter pants over my belly. My body, still thinking itself pregnant, had grown even while the baby hadn't. At the hospital I adjusted my gown so the doctor could sit by my knees. She was slender and graceful. Her long black hair looked disheveled. I wondered how long she had been awake.

"I'm sorry we are meeting under these circumstances," she said. "The procedure is simple. We will put you to sleep, dilate your cervix and apply light suction. Do you have any questions?"

I did, but didn't ask.

I woke to a nurse shouting my name and shaking my shoulder. She handed me a small plastic bowl of graham crackers and glass of apple juice. I couldn't stop chattering.

"It's time to go," she said. I rose gingerly, revealing a large pool of blood on the white bed linens.

"I'm sorry," I said.

For six weeks I lived in a state of limbo, believing that my womb was vacant, but having no verification. I had no bodily memory of the expulsion.

The doctor at my post-procedure check-up entered the room and reported enthusiastically, "Everything looks absolutely perfect!"

By perfect she meant empty.

"Just keep trying!"

I bled in the Amsterdam airport. I bled an hour before attending my friend's baby shower. I felt unfurnished and abandoned. I cried taking my nephews to the Children's Museum, as kids joyfully lapped around my legs. I cried at a baptism of someone else's baby. I felt forsaken and barren. I sat in my own pew during a family Ash Wednesday service and watched parents and children remind each other that they will be dust again someday. I felt cavernous and wanting. My uterus used to feel healthy, normal and powerful. Now it felt deserted and scraped bare. The hollowness was excruciatingly heavy.

We moved to Minneapolis and found an apartment with no mice. Grief wrapped itself around me and took hold. I walked through my days apart. My bones felt dehydrated. The silence started making a scraping sound. Somewhere I found the courage to ask for help. An intuitive healer I knew listened and seemed to understand the pain of invisible loss that exists outside the reach of our language. "You need witnesses and words to honor what happened," she said. She invited me to name the two babies. *Were they babies?*

Did they count? Am I a mother? She invited me to light two candles, to talk to the babies, to thank them for making me wiser and more compassionate in my brokenness, in my invisible scars, in my ethereal wounds. "Or plant a tree," she suggested, "anything tangible and visible that can be a witness to the life and loss."

I put both babies' due dates on my Google calendar to repeat annually. I bought a necklace with two interlocking squares, one slightly bigger than the other. I touched the squares to my throat several times a day. I pulled up the picture of the blue cross on my sink now and again and let myself weep. I grieved the babies and the anticipation of the babies. For a brief time, my body offered safety and warmth to something forming. For a few months, the sound of my heartbeat acted as a lullaby. I looked for them in the clouds and in the dirt and in the cool wind.

I started taking my basal temperature each morning. Dan brought me the thermometer while I remained warm under the covers. I decreased alcohol and caffeine as my normal. I took prenatal vitamins to keep me strong in the waiting. In the wilderness. Somedays I could convince myself that any hint of movement in my mid-section was a baby leaping inside me. Other days I cynically named it gas and moved on. I lived in two week cycles of ovulation and menstruation, hope and wanting.

Months later, in the middle of nothing in particular, I started crying and couldn't stop. I wandered into the bedroom and crumpled up in a fetal position on the bed. Dan gave me a few minutes and then cautiously approached me. He sat by my abdomen and gently caressed my upper back.

"What's wrong?" he whispered.

He should have known. Two lives carved out space and took up residence. Then they vacated. A million moments would never come to be. My ache echoed in the expanse. The sadness felt like waves, not words, and I was just too tired to translate them. I wasn't sure where even to begin.

"I don't know," I lied.

He made three more slow circles over my shoulder blades and then rose. "I'll make us some lunch," he offered and left.

5 AM

Jose Soares Braga

The alarm goes off. It's 5 a.m. Slowly, she opens her eyes. Near-total darkness around. She yawns and lifts her torso from the mattress that lies, frameless, on the floor, near the window. She peeks through the blinds' stripes. The city hasn't awoken yet. The night still engulfs civilization. With very slow movements, Cat opens a crack and feels a small breeze enter the hot, stuffy room. The scent of the city just before dawn invades the small space. In her mind, it almost smells like the aroma of the countryside on a rainy day. Even though there is no rain. Even though Cat is living in a residential area, on the outskirts of the capital city, far away from any sight of nature. She crawls out of her bed and stands up. While still in auto-pilot mode, she walks out of her room, through the small hallway, into the kitchen. She approaches the coffeemaker. In a few seconds, she grabs the first cup of coffee of the day.

Cat, short for Yekaterina, is a young woman with light-brown, curly hair, slightly above-average height. Her life in the city started about a year ago, when she moved in with two friends, after finishing her studies. Nowadays they work as freelance software developers. Before, even during college, she lived with her parents in a small rural town. She's always been very attached to her family, to her native place, to her childhood friends. Yet, her mind always traveled for her. Ever since her consciousness kicked in, Cat always travels to the farthest places around the world, and to the edge of the Universe. Ever since she remembers being herself, Cat has tried to uncover what could follow the end times, and what came before the Big Bang. The books she reads, the documentaries she watches, the conversations she has with interesting people, all have a major topic involved. Philosophy, religion, cosmology were always the bottom line issue. Politics and the arts were two of the other main topics other people like her liked to discuss and study. However, she didn't care much for those. They've always felt to her like a construction. Like there was something artificial about them. She could have felt the same about religion, for the same artificialness on the rituals and the mythology was as much a human construction as other "uninteresting" topics. Nevertheless, she could see there was something more in religion. Something inside every human being she knew, that told them there was something greater out there. That something was a conscient being of some sort. She often thought about life and death and the apparent meaninglessness of it all.

The first time in her life that she felt the effect of being high was not when she used drugs of any sort. It was not when she had the first contact with caffeine, or nicotine, or alcohol. It was before all of those experimentations that would come later in her life. She was only thirteen at the time. Her aunt had just passed away. As Cat sat down, during the wake, while ignoring the priest's words, the sadness of losing someone close to her, eventually evolved into something much deeper. She began questioning herself about death. If there was a life afterward, or even if there was a life before babies were born. What if there was no afterlife at all? Nobody knew what it was not to be alive. What it was not to be. As her mind grew more absent of surroundings, her consciousness traveled to the edge of existence for the first time. She tried to picture what it was not to be alive. It would be like sleeping without dreams. She imagined herself going through what her aunt did two days earlier. Closing her eyes for the last time. Taking her last breath. Entering the darkness. The deep void. Was that all? Only darkness? No. Darkness is something. Darkness is just turning off the lights. What Cat was experiencing was the absence of it all. Two seconds went by. She managed to experience only a moment of nothingness in her mind before simply crashing back into existence. Her eyes were dry and wide open. She let out a small moan and took a deep breath. Her mother asked her if she was ok. She said yes. She didn't know for sure, though, if that was an accurate answer. That simple episode had been life-changing. She still felt light-headed and was unsure about what to make of her experience. Through the years, she began acquiring some tools that would help her deal with her 'trip' to the edge of existence, but she was never satisfied. Life goes on. Eventually, she had to choose a degree in university. What she really wanted to major in was Philosophy, but her parents didn't support her choice. They forced her to choose a major that would imply she would get a good job. Her second choice, Physics and Mathematics, was also declined. Scientists don't make good money, they said. Finally, they all settled on Computer Science. Mom and Dad didn't know much about computers, but they were aware people could make a fortune in that area. At first, it seemed an odd choice for Yekaterina to pick something that didn't seem to fit in her worldview. However, the digital world also had its mysteries, its secrets, and was becoming more and more part of daily life in the first years of the 21st Century. The infancy of the web seemed to be in the past already and a new and unsure future was unraveling before the very eyes of humanity.

Cat found her place in academia, graduated, and moved near the capital city to find her place in reality. Now, at the age of 23, she is living with her friends, Anton and Vladislav. All of them work enough to make a good living, especially since they are sharing rent in an apartment on one of the most reasonably priced parts of the outskirts in a former Soviet republic. Life is very cheap. She works in the morning and they work through the night. During the late afternoon, they usually do something together. Watch a movie, play videogames, have a nice dinner party with other friends, or go out drinking. Life is good for all of them but, after a year, it has fallen into an almost inflexible routine. Cat feels there is something more she needs from life. Her life is happy but seems empty.

As Cat walks into the living room, the darkness starts to slowly fade away. It's not a very large space, but it's enough to hold a couch, a television, and the three small desks that make up the small home office where they work. Occupying one of the places, sits Anton, sleeping, with his head buried in his arms. Vladislav must have gone to bed, not long before.

"Tupoy baran," she murmurs to herself.

Cat starts poking Anton's chair with her foot.

"Chto? Mama?"

"I'm not your *mama*, Anton. Go to bed."

"Grrmgh...bed..."

Anton gets up and slowly walks toward his room. Cat takes a sip of her coffee and walks to the window. A new day is dawning in the city. Old, damaged, Soviet-style apartment buildings are the norm outside. On the ground, some trees, dirty sidewalks, and small, badly-kept, grass-littered parks. A single picnic table and two benches stand, abandoned, in the middle of one of those small green areas. In an hour or two, usually, three or four babushki get together and drink some spirit-lifting beverages, while talking about life.

Cat sits down at her computer. The program she's been working on is a simple accounting software for a small company. Not a lot of work, not worth a gigantic amount of money, but more than enough to keep her lifestyle. Yet, it is boring work.

After her self-imposed shift ends, she decides to take a walk around town, maybe grab a bus into the center.

A quick shower and a half-an-hour ride later, she arrives at the capital's historic center. Her day's labor is over for the day, but all the other citizens seem to either be already at work or going there. Traffic jams, crowds of people crossing roads and rushing through sidewalks, like ants roaming around after a lump of sugar falls on the floor. The historical center is a mix of old, centenary, restored buildings, and a few recent ones. Eventually, Cat reaches her destination, a large, modern, two-story coffee shop. She sits near the window, on the top floor. Resting comfortably, she watches life unraveling outside. People seem stressed, busy, unhappy. Most of them have the same routine. Sleep-work-sleep, for most of their lives, with a few breaks in between. Then, death. Quite a pointless life, she bitterly thinks. She is lucky to not have to dedicate most of her life to a pointless job. Some of the work she does is, indeed, pointless, but usually, she enjoys it. She does enjoy the great amount of free time she has. Notwithstanding, there is always something missing. What was the point of it all? The small moments, perhaps. Enjoying a small walk. Waking up early before anyone else and watching the sunrise. Or the big moments. Going back home to spend time with her loved ones. Partying with her friends and not caring about the hangover that would strike the following morning. Finding love and having kids. Should happiness be the reason for a life that seems so pointless in the end? Some people find the reason to live in religion. Those people seem to, at least, have a purpose in life. Still, there is always something that seems fake about religion. Perhaps it was due to her family not taking their faith too seriously. They believed in God but didn't make Him part of their daily life. Cat grew up without a strong divine presence around. She didn't find it necessary for the world to have been created by someone or something. Even if there is such a powerful being on the origin of existence, that doesn't mean there would be life after death. You only live on as a part of other natural organisms after you die. However, most people would not be content with that ending, for their essence of being would be wiped out of the face of the earth. That is not a fun destiny for people who spent their entire life working meaningless jobs. Or enjoying themselves. Or helping others. That is not a fun ending for anyone. Some say the memories that we leave in others is the true meaning of life. Nonsense. Eventually, nobody will remember anybody from nowadays. A select few will be part of history books, and a great part of it will be pure fiction. Some say being born is in itself a statistical miracle.

If a great-great-grandmother failed to meet a great-great-grandfather, their great-great-grandson would have never existed. Our conscient being exists. But why?

Cat doesn't even notice she has already eaten her snack and nearly finished her *latte*. She doesn't feel well. Something is wrong. All her life she knew something *felt* wrong. Now, that feeling is growing stronger. Gazing through the window, she sees fewer people on the street. Suddenly, she notices one man, standing still. A short man, with a brownish skin tone, glasses, and very dark hair. He's staring at her. Something feels very wrong, now.

The alarm goes off. It's 5 AM. Slowly, she opens her eyes. Near-total darkness around. She yawns and lifts her torso from the mattress that lies, frameless, on the floor near the window. She peeks through the blinds' stripes. The city... isn't there anymore. There's a beach, instead. It seems like the sun will be rising soon. She opens the window and looks outside. The scent of the city night is gone. It smells like something she's never smelled before. It's probably the smell of the ocean. She looks back into the room. It's her room. The same room she's been living in the past year. However, it's no longer located on the 7th floor of a building on the outskirts of the capital city. It's on the ground floor of a beach house. "I must still be dreaming," she wonders. Dumbfounded, she sits on the edge of her bed, expressionless. After a few seconds, she hears a knock on the door.

"Who's there?" She queries.

"A friend," a soft, unknown voice says while opening the door.

The glasses-wearing man from outside of the coffeeshop enters the room. Cat starts to remember the last hour before everything went away. She was looking outside to the people in the square and she saw that same man looking straight at her. She remembers feeling uneasy. Now, she feels the same way.

"Don't worry, Cat. I'm not here to hurt you."

"What did you do to me? Did you drug me?"

"I didn't drug you," he says. "Do you like your new ocean view? Much more pleasant than those old buildings."

"What happened? Who are you?"

"I'm the one who created the universe you lived at."

"What? You're...God?"

"I guess you can put it that way."

"This is insane. I don't believe you."

"But you will. We don't have to be here. Come."

Before Cat can reply, her room, dimly lit by the rising sun outside disappears and both of them start floating. They're not surrounded by darkness, for she can clearly see herself and the strange man, but everything else seems to be a complete void. This is the (non-)place she managed to enter, for a couple of seconds, back when she was a teenager.

"This feels familiar, doesn't it?"

"I can't believe this."

"But you're starting to."

"If you're really God, why did you show up to me? Did I die?"

"You didn't die. Quite the contrary, actually. You're a survivor. And why you? Because I think you're very interesting and wanted to have a chat."

"You wanted to have a chat with me? Ok. So, you're the 'Almighty', the 'King of Kings', the 'Alpha and the Omega'..."

"Sure, sure, but you can call me Jim-Bob."

Cat immediately bursts into laughter.

"I'm sorry, God... Jim-Bob. Sorry! That's just... I didn't realize..."

"That's ok. I'm just a normal guy, you know? I'm not used to being seen as a divinity."

"Where are we, Jim-Bob? How am I a survivor?"

"Before I tell you where we are, I should explain where you came from. Your reality and everything in it is a computer program that I created. Your whole life, all the events that occurred long before you were alive and that have occurred long after you've passed are a part of a simulation. The artificial intelligence developed in the software managed to attribute consciousness to every living being. Every cell and organism that exists has its own capacity to be aware of the self. And you are part of that reality."

"Wow. Ok. This is too much for me to process. So... I'm no more than a bunch of lines of text on a computer?"

"You are a bunch of self-aware cells that were created in a digital Big Bang originated by a bunch of lines of text on a computer. Your universe was made in the image of my own. You and I are both humans. Even our history is very similar to your history."

"Fair enough. And why am I a survivor?"

"Well, I kind of ruined most of your universe by mistake."

"You what? Why? How?"

"I was clumsy. I spilled Coca-Cola on the drive that was running your program."

"What's Coca-Cola?"

"A soda. You don't have it in your realm. Only Pepsi."

"Ah, ok. Wait, is that why I'm here, in the void, with you? You destroyed my world... with soda?!"

"Kind of. You're here because I wanted to talk to you. I'm able to talk with you because not all of the code was gone. I made backups of some people, places, elements. When you saw me outside the coffee shop, I was making a backup of your conscience. Moments ago, we were talking inside a small beach simulator and now we're on an empty program. Don't worry, I'm working on fixing everything. You'll be back living your life in no time."

"Can we go somewhere else? It feels weird to be here, floating, surrounded by literally nothing."

All of a sudden, both of them are transported to the beach she saw through her window. The sun is still rising. Not a minute has gone by since they left. Now, they are outside. Cat is bare-footed, feeling the sand as she walks around. She could see the landscape now. A large body of very clean water, ending in the floor made out of sand, that extends, past the small beach house her room was in, into the distance, ending far away, into a mountain range. Experiencing for the first time the feeling of being on a beach, she walks side-by-side with Jim-Bob, in total silence, for a few moments.

"I'll be honest, Cat. There is a reason I chose to talk to you, from the countless life forms created in your universe."

"I'm listening."

"When you pictured the absolute void, you 'peeked' outside of the simulation. That wasn't supposed to have happened. You're the only being that has a conscience developed to the point of reaching outside the realms of my creation. You are special, Cat."

"That's a nice way of saying that I'm a bug in your software."

"In a way. But you're an interesting bug. Not only are you unique in your reality, you are also more interesting than anybody I know from my world."

"Do you know what is going to happen to me in the future?"

"No. I know what would happen to you in the old simulation. Now, you are outside of the program, and the program is gone. Like I said, I'm creating a new one."

"I... don't think I want to go live in another simulation, Jim-Bob. I want to live in your world."

"How come?"

"It's not real. I'm not real. Somehow I always knew I wasn't real and you just confirmed it."

"You are real, Cat. The universe that generated what you are is real. The only difference is that your reality was generated artificially inside another reality."

Cat gets silent and starts thinking about what Jim-Bob just said. Both keep walking in silence, on the sand, near the ocean.

"Then...," Cat resumes, "Where did you come from?"

"Me? From my parents..."

"Oh, come on, dude, seriously? I mean, where did your people, your universe come from?"

"I dunno. The Big Bang, I guess. We still don't know what came before time started or what started time."

"Is it possible that your universe is also just a computer program generated by another 'Jim-Bob'?

"Huh... I guess." A few seconds go by. "This is why I wanted to speak to you. I knew this was going to be a very interesting interaction."

"Thank you."

"What if..."

"Yes, Jim-Bob?"

"What if we're all just a bunch of simulations that generate other simulations, that generate other simulations, and so on? I know that in your world, you eventually got the technology to generate an AI as advanced as in my world."

"Interesting. I wonder if that is the reason we exist. Would that be the meaning of life? To create other realities?"

"Maybe. Maybe not. Do you really need life to have meaning? Why can't we just be?"

"I don't know. I guess we'll never know."

"Look, Cat. I can't do what you asked me. You can't just simply 'come to live' in my reality. I have a counter-proposal for you, though."

"I'm listening."

"I could get you back to a universe similar, in everything, to your own, but also give you the technology you need to develop simulations of other universes. Would you care for that?"

"I guess."

"Always remember, Yekaterina. You are as real as I am."

The alarm goes off. It's 5 a.m. Slowly, she opens her eyes. Near-total darkness around. She yawns and lifts her torso from the mattress that lies, frameless, on the floor near the window. She peeks through the blinds' stripes. The city is there, once again. In a few minutes, Cat will be back on her computer, working on her new project. Now, she is more than just 'Cat, the programmer'. She is the 'Almighty', the 'Queen of Queens', the 'Alpha and the Omega'

ADMIRALACKBARINTHENIGHTKINGSARMY
Terry Wright
Medium: Digital on canvas
Dimensions: 36x48

WIDOW'S WALK

Cynthia Trenshaw

She's found no tourniquet to staunch the pain
that ferments, torments, hollows out her day;
no comfort but the widow's walk, again.

Not gabled roof, but carpet pile, sustains
the worn-down path that keeps madness at bay.
She's found no other way to staunch the pain.

Cards expressing sympathy contain
not balm, but manufactured, cheap cliché.
No comfort but the widow's walk, again.

Her beloved's final breaths remain
haunting memory, gasps of gray.
She's found no tourniquet to staunch that pain.

Decades of other widows' whispers strain
to empathize this pacing passion play:
"No comfort but the widow's walk, again."

It seems she's logged a thousand miles and gained
Nowhere. Wrung out. Still here, and yet astray.
She's found no tourniquet to staunch the pain,
"no comfort but the widow's walk, again."

IN SEARCH OF AN EXIT

jd hegarty

It feels like I have never slept.
Every time my eyes get heavy,

Rod Serling appears in my living room,
looks directly through me, and rattles

off a pithy line about the logic of twilight,
but he cannot pull me through a dimension

of mind and shadow. The logic of this is fascism.
We watch children put into cages

and retweet and scroll and scroll and Rod
watches us, trying not to judge, but how

can he not? He wanted us to make a pitch
for the angels. The hashtag resistance

couldn't sell water in hell. They remind us
there is a gremlin on the wing of the plane,

but they don't try to land the plane.
Rod thought we would travel the stars,

but not like this. Not at the expense of
each other. Our leaders belong on a prison planet.

The capitalists sing the body electric because
the demands of a human body are too much

for them. We are obsolete. Sometimes
there is a moral, but mostly, Rod stares

us down as we watch ourselves twist
and writhe. As we see the twists coming,

but can do nothing to stop the twisting. He
tells us stories about war and we are always at war

and we are always debating the morality of
how to fight a war, but not the why. And death

is always following behind us, hoping to be
welcomed. We question everything. We question

how to serve man. We think about silence.
We think about violence. We ask Rod for

answers and he simply tells us that things
are strange here at the intersection

of apathy and technology, underneath
the shadow of foolishness. All of this

becomes cruelty. All of this is quest for power.

Rod Serling cannot save us. Neither can he

guide us out. We are not merely passing
through here. The foundations are built

from this shadowstuff. We were born here
and will die so many times here

before we learn anything about how
to love each other, how to show a quality of mercy,

and there will never, never be time.

ON MY FATHER'S SUICIDE

Joette Varnado

East Texas, 2011

This piece of land looks like a scab and the tall
weeds, having never known green, bow towards
me while I crunch along. The air cottoning my mouth
tastes like gunpowder and gasoline. Now deep
in cicada country, their gradual crescendo
and decrescendo sounds like the breaths that
come before sleep, like a rain that never quiets.
When I reach the shack where he used to live,
a vulture loiters on a dying elm tree beside it, staring
at me approaching him. I wonder if this bird,
hunched and tired, saw my father die in this place.
How long did he watch him kneel here in this
yard, teeth clamped on dense barrel, before he
lurched, alone, a distant rumbling in the open sky;
the only witness of his passing? A lit match,
certainly no one can see from space, going out.
Does he remember the taste of him, rotten bone
marrow and flesh steeping in the grass on which I
now stand, looking up at the same eyes that saw it
happen? Did he taste a stomach-churning evil
rank enough to hoard the carcass from any other
death-hungry creature? Did the word *rapist* stain

his beak, his tongue? Was it too hard to eat? Did
it leak her name, my babysitter? Did the ground
shrug with relief, grateful for my father's quick
untethering? Can I look up at this greying
bird, watch him finally fly away, and continue,
like this place, this air, this eroding land, to breathe?

EACH HAZY ELEMENT LOOKING FOR CONNECTION

Joanne Nelson

This is about my dad's basement den, his toy car collection, and my engagement. Or so it seems anyway—these three things circling each other for weeks now, each hazy element looking for connection.

First, my engagement in the late 1980s. My boyfriend of six years finally asked me to marry him. He scheduled a weekend getaway, made reservations at a fancy restaurant, brought along a single rose he forgot to give me, even got down on one knee. Despite our many years together, the decision to join our lives in front of God and everybody made us both giddy, and each announcement to friends and family brought me a rush of joy, of possibility.

I couldn't wait to tell my father. Not because we were close or because I thought he'd desire a role; but because, in this new blush of potentiality, my existence was corrupted by glossy images from bride magazines. Myself and my father as photo opportunity more than as two real people with twenty-eight years of history.

"Can't tonight," he told me when I called and asked to stop over. He and my stepmother, Delores, were busy, maybe another time.

No, no. That's okay. Nothing important.

We scheduled time to visit them the next week. Our enthusiasm just a smidge dimmed; although I held onto his rejection as if it were purposeful. As though a space had opened between my excitement and this particular telling that I could fill with scripted assumptions for years to come.

Maybe the enthusiasm was *somewhat* more than a smidge dimmed.

Now I recognize his need to buffer in distance between emotions and events. During my freshman year in high school, a year or so after leaving our home to take up with his current wife, he'd sometimes park down the block in his shiny red car to drive me to school. I remember feeling a stomach-achy rush of fear when I spotted his car. Not because of anything untoward in his relationship with me, but because of how my mother would handle knowledge of our seeing each other. Her hurt at his betrayal was endless and I became her living, breathing, always present representative of injury. I suppose we commented on the weather or the long wait between buses while we journeyed down Oklahoma Avenue all the way to St. Mary's Academy; but my clearest memories are of the sound of the door as I pulled it closed, vinyl seats in a car that had never been part of our family, and his pleasant "Hey, Kid" as I settled in, before he returned his gaze to the road. Neither of us ever remarked on his surprise appearance or the change in his living arrangements.

I recognize my own complicity, the way I also turned my eyes to the street winding out of our neighborhood instead of initiating any meaningful conversation. I knew how to hold my tongue. On the day he'd filled his car with boxes and moved out, he asked me if I'd miss him and I didn't say a word in reply, protecting him from my answer.

As expected, Dad led us to his den the night of our scheduled visit. He had a black leather easy chair where no one sat except him, a comfortable couch, a television, and a door, mere feet from his chair, that opened to an old staircase now used to store beer. The den's paneled walls were crowded with handmade display cases filled with his toy car collection. Toy cars—over 600 of them—that even his grandchildren knew existed for looking, not for touching. A separate vitrine housed decanters of whiskey-filled porcelain Indy 500 race cars (their value questionable since my mother had broken the seal of each before handing them over in the divorce settlement). The driver's names stenciled on the cars felt like old friends: Foyt, Unser, Andretti.

These were the drivers I rooted for on Sunday afternoons when my parents and I gathered around the television, window shades pulled down to prevent glare, and watched the races—any conversation angrily hushed, the spell of the engine roar not to be broken. Despite the dark, enforced silence, I savored these long afternoons spent together. I devoted my time to drawing in the Indianapolis 500 coloring book he'd bought me, careful to stay in the lines, looking up if the announcer's voice rose in anticipation of an accident.

The glass cases of miniatures in his current home intrigued me the most. Some diecast replicas came with functional parts and white rubber wheels graced the oldest models. A deep blue Model A had a working rumble seat of red, a tractor had a moveable hitch. Roadsters and pickups and Thunderbirds and Mustangs, even the occasional Buick Electra, lined shelf after shelf on all sides of the room. My grandmother once told me what a good boy he—my dad, her son—was if she bought him a toy car to hold while they shopped. Quiet and content in his stroller, he'd turn the wheels around and around.

Little of the actual announcing of our engagement to him remains clear. Just our phone call, driving to his house the next week, and being in that room with all the cars watching us. Delores probably brought pretzels down from the kitchen while we settled onto the couch and he poured Pabst. What fogs the words of our conversation is the variety of fictions I created about the visit both before and after our arrival. My dad, I worried, questioned our need to interrupt a perfectly good evening with something best accomplished over the phone. But I'd wanted to see his expression when we made our announcement—although I don't recall what I wanted his expression to be or even what it actually was. It's as if, in his small den, we each sat in a different car headed in a different direction: my dad with a need to drive away, me with a need to arrive.

Delores mostly kept herself busy in other rooms during our visits. I suppose we asked her to stay. Maybe she felt embarrassed to hear of our engagement—what could she, or my father, share of their history? My grandmother had told me the story of my parents' marriage. How he went AWOL from his army unit for the hasty, necessary wedding—which his own father refused to attend. And this current marriage? Dad shared his nuptial news in a phone call weeks after the event; like describing a hiccup in his schedule, certainly nothing requiring a visit or an announcement.

Happier stories existed. I'd come across a 1964 photo of him at the wheel of his restored Ford Model A, a just-married cousin and her husband waving from the rumble seat. I wonder if he thought about that day while we discussed our plans. He'd have detailed the Model A with tenderness. I knew this from a childhood of watching him prepare for parades and car shows—the round can of Turtle Wax always close, the refusal of any offers of help, the way he'd lift us kids into the rumble seat to avoid getting the slightest of fingerprints on the Brewster green finish.

Family members had often accused my dad of caring more about cars than us. Perhaps serving as chauffeur for the bride and groom afforded him the opportunity to quiet the charge. I think he relished his separation from the din and emotion of wedding well-wishers—sequestered in the cabin of his model A, the newlyweds behind him all but forgotten.

Except for the toy cars still lining his walls, the den is empty now. The furniture has been passed on to others, the television given away. A combination of mustiness and mildew hangs in the air, dust gathers wherever it can. My dad is dead and won't celebrate my thirtieth anniversary or learn of my own daughter's engagement. Delores transitioned to an apartment and no longer drives, the couple from the rumble seat divorced long ago. So many arrivals and departures from his room of toy cars. Now it is only the possibility; no, only the desire to drive away that is left.

Such a shame, really, to have all those wheels remain so still.

OF STARS AND JOYCE AND THE INTERLUDE OF THE BIG NIGHT CAT

Elaine Guo

It was September, and one night there were two full moons in the sky. Curious, I stepped out onto my balcony, feeling the chill of the stone seep into my feet, and looked up above the winking city skyline. The moons blinked at me.

I paused. Then I blinked back. It seemed the only polite thing to do. Another pause. A crater on each moon began to darken and grow, and soon I was staring at eyes with almonds for pupils. Of course they were eyes. They had blinked at me.

"What are you?" I whispered, in my head or out loud, it did not matter. The owner of the eyes purred in answer. A line the shape of Mr. Monopoly's moustache spread across the sky and shimmered against the indigo night as if it were the portal to the Milky Way.

I stared. Mr. Monopoly's moustache yawned. At once the moons were crescents, and they grew and grew, and then for a moment I was staring at nothing but stars. When I had blinked away the flashes behind my retinas, I found a cat with moonlight eyes and a Milky Way smile sitting on the railing. He had fur the color snow takes on just when dusk is fading to night and a tail bent into a right angle near the tip. I had never seen a bigger cat in my life. I turned back to the sky. There was no more moon.

I opened the door to my room to let him in. He leapt without a sound onto my bed.

At this point in the proceedings someone else might come to the conclusion that they were going mad; or at least were hallucinating. Neither was happening to me, and I could be certain because I was already mad. This was a fact I had known for exactly four years and there could be no argument. What sort of child did not cry even once following her father's death? Only a mad one.

My mother thought so. She never asked why I did not cry. I think she recognized madness when she saw it.

I sank into bed and stroked the silkiness of the cat's head, wondering what to call him. His purpleness lit a bulb, and a sly grin spread across my face. He grinned back, his smile shimmering.

"You're Tom. How's that?" I asked. "I'm not getting a Jerry mouse for you to chase around, but I think you're Tom."

Tom blinked at me. He did not think much of the name.

"It'll grow on you."

Tom yawned, and in his open mouth I saw more stars than I'd ever seen in the New York City sky.

I picked him up. He weighed nothing.

"Well, if you're going to stay, I'll just go show you to Mom so she doesn't freak when she sees you." Walking toward my bedroom door, the corner of my eye caught something in the mirror. I froze, one leg just above the carpet. Sure that I was mistaken, I inched my head around to stare at my reflection. My reflection did not show a cat in my arms.

I looked up at the mirror, then down at Tom, then up at the mirror again. My reflection looked rather stupid, holding on to nothingness. I put Tom back on my bed.

"I guess only I can see you, huh?"

He rolled his head in a lazy, derisive sort of way, then turned around and stretched.

"Right. Sorry I'm so slow in catching on."

In the following weeks Tom followed me everywhere, an extension of my shadow. Or my limbs. At school, in class, he coiled and twined his body around my ankles and spent the days pawing at the patches of light the shifting trees outside made dance on the classroom floor. I did not know why Tom was here. The moon had not returned to the sky.

At night, after homework and volleyball and dinner with a mother who, these days, laughed liked a teenager, I lay on my stomach and tried to read James Joyce.

I had been trying to read *Ulysses* for four years, and was on Chapter VI.

I couldn't remember who Cunningham was. No doubt I'd missed something along the way, but there was also no way in Hades I was going back and rereading. I soldiered on. What the hell were gasworks? More talking. More characters I didn't remember. There should be a law against the existence of the word "quiff."

The text was beginning to tangle into lines of yarn beyond salvation when Tom jumped onto my book.

"Get off." I swatted at him. He did not budge.

"Come on, at least let me get through ten pages." He did not budge. I went to pick him up, but he was a sneaky pest. Before I knew it, Tom had nudged the book off my bed and picked it up with his mouth. With a mutinous flick of his head, he sent the book flying against my balcony door. Then he sat on it like a melting grape popsicle and looked at me with testy moon eyes.

"Fine. Fine. I'll go to bed then."

That night I had The Dream again. The one I always did. The one in which Dad came back, but someone else's father was dead. This time the dead dad was Mr. Moreland, who lived next door. His triplet sons were seven. I tried to be sorry. I wasn't.

It was October, and Tom had taken an unwholesome interest in my betta fish, who lived on my nightstand. Back when I wanted to be a photographer, Dad had gotten me the fish so I could practice taking photos of its ever-swirling skirts. I named him Mr. T. after Mr. Tiffany. Because he was blue.

Tom's attentions to Mr. T. were giving me a tick. I kept turning my head whenever I saw a purple flash near by bed, so eventually I moved his bowl to the high bookshelf against my window. Tom surveilled me with narrowed crescent eyes, then took some moments to decide if the fish was interesting enough to warrant a jump up the shelves. He was not. Mr. T.'s new home would be the bookshelf against the window.

Satisfied, I was mid-flop onto my bed when my mother walked in. She had on a dress the color I had always imagined mermaid earwax to be. It was sequined, but the sequins were placed just far enough apart that the fabric underneath was clearly visible. Shimmery earwax on matte, if you will. At first I thought she had dyed some strands of her hair teal to match the dress, but realized that I was only seeing the spaghetti straps. She did paint her eyelids to match her dress though. It looked like her eyes were framed by two thick veins.

"I'm just heading out for the night, sweetheart," she said, her smile stretching her cheeks wider than her forehead. "Don't wait up."

After Dad died, my mother had morphed into a slutty college freshman. This turn of events wasn't altogether unpleasant, but some mornings I would find the residue of her one night stand drinking coffee in the kitchen of our townhouse.

I gave her a kiss and forced my lips to curl up. I deserved to make a request. "Have fun, mom," I said. "Can you just tell whoever you bring home to have their morning coffee in the upstairs dining room?"

"Whatever you want, dear. Good niiiiight." she sang the word like a doorbell and left my room. The next morning, I didn't have to enter the kitchen to hear the sound of coffee mug on marble counter. I left without breakfast.

It was November, and I was still reading Chapter VI. There was something about a funeral. I could make out that much. Then there seemed to be a letter of some importance. I didn't know what jarvies were. "He went very suddenly" did he? "The best death" was it? The macabre bit of my brain that liked to pull at scabs for fun wondered if Dad thought about this funeral scene that morning. When he knew there was no getting out. When he knew he was going to die.

Then it wondered why, out of all the enchanting, mesmerizing, soul-wrenching novels out there, Dad had liked this goddamned book so much. Why did he always have to talk about *this fucking book*? Couldn't he have had another favorite? Something normal? So I wouldn't have to lie here now and read nonsense?

There was a paw on my face. This was joined by another paw. The pads of Tom's paws were warm compresses over my swollen eyes. It seemed cats with Milky Way smiles did not have claws.

"Get off me." I shoved him away. He returned and this time launched his entire body at my head. Now all I could see was the lavender fur of his tummy.

"Can you just let me get halfway through the chapter?" In answer, he maneuvered his back leg and kicked the book out of my hands, then returned to settling on my face.

"So, no?" My voice sounded wooly against his soft neck. He hit my arm with his crooked tail.

That night I had The Dream again. Dad was back, alive, just like he should be. Except this time, it was my mother who was dead. I tried very hard to be sorry. I wasn't.

Nobody likes November. Not really. The world of November is washed out and faded. The moon had yet to return to the sky, but no one seemed to notice. November will do that to you. Make you forget the moon.

One day I opened my bedroom door and could not move. The straps of my book bag were gnawing into my fingers but I could not move. The pale yellow of November afternoon was reaching through my window and into the fishbowl housing Mr. T. Light flooded the water and fell through the flowing skirts of his tail, sprinkling blue crepuscular rays about my desk and carpet. I dropped my bag on my foot. It didn't even hurt.

I crept to my closet, eyes fixed on the fishbowl, as if one wrong move would disturb the light beast and chase it away forever. I knew exactly where to reach, though I hadn't touched the bag in four years, and retrieved my camera from its hiding place. My unsighted hands knew how to replace the lens. My eyes were needed to keep watch over the light.

There had been a time I wanted to be a photographer. When the camera was new. When the millennium was new. I was twelve and I knew what I wanted. But then I was wrong. Now I wanted to be a lawyer. It took more time and study than was healthy to be a lawyer. Dad had always said so. So if I wanted to be a lawyer, there would be no time to be a photographer. I'd put my camera away.

But surely, today, I could be a photographer. Just for a bit. Just for this hour. November surely would not show me this light just to taunt me.

I shot until I ran out of film. I discovered angles of my bedroom I never knew existed. And after all the clicks, the god rays of Tiffany blue were still swimming on my carpet, so I lay on my stomach and watched them. Tom stretched himself out between my shoulder blades.

It was January, and there was a boy I wanted. He played lacrosse. He was a feminist. His name was James, and he had very mischievous eyes. I had never wanted anything so badly. My friends told me he wasn't over his ex. That was alright. I could give him time. But he was the boy I wanted and there was no reason I should be denied. Whoever was out there, making the decisions—they owed me.

In January, it only ever snows at night. In December the skies are white and snow swirls from nothingness into nothingness, but January snow arrives only in blizzards, and the world is so dark that even white is not white. No one seemed surprised, then, that the moon had still yet to appear in the sky. Tom disappeared at night now, into the snow, I assumed. Maybe cats with the galaxies shimmering through their teeth liked to sit in the stinging, swarming blizzard. And yet the moon had not returned.

I lost my copy of *Ulysses*. I could not pinpoint the exact day, but when I made up my mind to attempt it once more, it was nowhere to be found. I knew Tom had hidden it. Or maybe he had tossed it into the snow. I even asked him, more than once, where the book had gone, but he just looked at me with innocent moonlight eyes that told me I was an idiot.

My friends asked me why I liked James so much. I giggled in that despotic way teenaged girls giggle, as if all that mattered was my amusement in that flicker of a second, and told them "how would I know? I just want him." They giggled too, and said a great many pretty things that I liked to hear. Not that I needed to hear them. The Somewhere Out There owed this to me.

Tom did not like James. Sometimes, when we saw him with his lacrosse team, Tom would try to jump on my head and blind me with his paws. Sometimes he bared his shimmering little fangs. Mostly, he stole my flip phone when he knew who I was texting. He would paw it away from my hands and dangle it from the corner of his mouth like some decomposing animal as he walked away. I did not know if Tom disapproved of James as a human, or if I did not have a reason for wanting him.

I went downtown one Saturday with just my camera. I made sure it was cold before leaving home, and made sure not to wear too many layers. The wind would bite and claw at my skin, and it would sting, and I would make it through the day riding on the high of the bone-piercing cold.

All afternoon I stared at the construction happening in the monstrous pit that was Ground Zero. And kept wondering where all the rubble went. And whether someone had been responsible for sifting through the lost shoes and broken picture frames to determine if they could be returned to the families. I never got Dad's shoe.

It was March, and I was at another party in an apartment whose owner I did not know. Friend of a friend of a friend, or something like that. Maybe I did know her. Everyone knew too much about everyone else in the city anyway.

I was kissing a boy whose name I couldn't remember. Later in the night I let him have sex with me on my floor. I turned my head and there it was, my copy of *Ulysses* lying under the bed.

The next morning Tom returned from his nightly frolic and found me again trying to finish Chapter VI. There was too much Latin in this book. I was approaching five years of mandatory school Latin and still I understood nothing. No one sane had time for this. I registered the word "maggots". Why must every human state be revolting? Life was full of unpalatable interludes, but even death could not be clean. "A corpse is meat gone bad…cremation better… ashes to ashes…" Does it still count if you turn to ashes in a ball of fire you didn't ask for? I wondered if Dad's copy of *Ulysses* had turned to ashes with him. Maybe his shoes were ashes too.

It became clear that Tom had hidden my book under the bed. He did not like that I had it back. This time he resorted to a coercive tactic. He sat on my back and stuck his bent tail under my nose. I brushed it aside. The tail returned. I brushed it aside. Again, it returned. Somehow, every time his tail returned it became fluffier. I sneezed, and my eyes lost my spot on the page. Another thought lost. Another broken string of concentration.

"You're not going to let this go, are you?"

His tail, despite the bend, made a slow, graceful wave in the air. He pushed a paw into the cover of my book, and it closed shut.

"You are a tyrant, you know that?" A shimmering smile.

Tom stopped disappearing into the night.

It was April, and I was in James' living room, wiping his coffee table with a paper towel possibly wet with beer. He'd hosted a party. I'd stayed to help him clean.

At one point in the evening there had been more wine in me than blood, I was sure, and he was drunker, and that was good. But now the air was blue again, and my skin was cold, and we sat on his coffee table, both too sober to move our faces.

At last he thanked me for staying to help, and I thought if I did not kiss him now I may as well never do anything again. From the corner of my eye I caught a glimpse of a shimmering fang. I ignored it with conviction.

James was slow to push me away, and when he did his hand was still on my neck.

"No, that's not—I don't like you like that." He removed his hand.

I shrugged. "I'm not asking you to marry me." Then I pulled my sweater off over my head. "I just want…this."

He took a long, brittle breath and ran a nervous hand in his hair.

"I mean…No, I don't want this sort of hook up thing either." He took a step back from me.

I blinked. And again. And again.

"Why don't you want me?" I whispered, though I was not sure if I said anything aloud.

"Claudia? I'm sorry if I—"

"No." My voice was barely human, hollow and metallic. What did one say to this kind of apology?

"No, don't tell me you're sorry."

And the vast imbalances of the cosmos seemed to crystalize on the hubris of my soul and melt through my eyes like they had not done for years and years until I was crying and crying and shaking and could not stop.

Couldn't I just have this?

At three in the morning I sat in my bathtub and listened to the water thunder as it filled. My body felt empty, like all the blood had rushed to my face and escaped in the form of tears. I shut my eyes against the muted bathroom light, too gentle, and perhaps I slept, but did not dream The Dream again.

I was sitting on a bench, under a sky alive with stars, and beside me sat my father in a morning suit and red bowtie. He removed his stiff top hat and raised an eyebrow, as if seeking my approval. His black silk hat was as tall as a cake. I stared into his face, which I told myself was familiar, and yet seemed foreign and new.

"Dad, you look ridiculous."

"Claudia, I'm dead. I can wear what I want." From his other hand he produced a fake white moustache and stuck it on his lip. Then he looked towards the stars and in an instant everything was different. In the sky were billions of Technicolor orbs so close I swore I could touch them and constellations whose shapes did not exist in this world.

I turned to him, to ask if he had noticed, but then he spoke, still looking at the sky,

"This is what the universe really looks like."

"Oh." I paused. "So, before…"

"That was the way I arranged it."

"Can you put it back?"

He smiled and waved his hand, and the stars returned, shimmering like the tooth of a cat.

"It won't stick, though. It'll fall away, and you'll end up with the real deal. No matter how hard you try."

And then I was staring at galaxies within Tom's yawning mouth. I turned off the faucet.

Beside me lay my copy of *Ulysses,* and I opened it to the end of Chapter VI. Oyster eyes indeed, after that eruption of crying… But thank you, nonetheless... for how grand it all began to feel.

I let the book fall into the water.

It was May, and one night there was a full moon in the sky.

POPPY
Meredith Field
Medium: Acrylic
Dimensions: 16x24 oval

Editors' Choice

AT HOME WITH MY HERBAL REMEDY AND HIS BOOKS

Dvora Wolff Rabino

Home is where my husband is. My second husband, Herb: the one I met when I was a divorced mom in my 40s, the one I quickly came to call my Herbal Remedy. Now, years later, his deep-sunk eyes remind me of an elephant's: ancient, steady and wise. I trace with my index finger the crinkles fanning out from their fleshy corners. I nuzzle against his neck, sniffing his indefinable but still-tantalizing aroma. When we lie down, I rest my head on his chest. He strokes my head and arms and holds me. His "good night" gently rumbles, vibrating the strings of my heart. Unlike me, he falls asleep effortlessly, immediately, guiltlessly. His quiet breaths and soft moans become my long, slow lullaby.

Herb's waters are still, deep, and sometimes well concealed, for he is a historian and philosopher, and his is primarily a world of ideas. The bookshelves lining his upstairs study are so overcrowded with heavy tomes that we had to hire a contractor to reinforce the dining room ceiling below. Obscuring the entire surface of his massive desktop are philosophy articles, medical journal abstracts, sociological and political analyses, and more law review articles than I have read in my entire legal career. Recent issues of *The New York Times,* the London, Jewish, and New York Reviews of Books, *the Journal of Medical Ethics, The Atlantic, The Nation, The New Yorker, Jacobin, and Science Magazine* occupy much of our dining table real estate and are stacked high on a couple of the chairs beside it. On the living room coffee table sit a tractate of the Talmud and several books of Biblical commentaries. Flyers from Jews for Racial and Economic Justice, The Centre for Alternative Technology, and—for good measure—the CATO Institute are spread out on the kitchen counters. Conveniently atop Herb's bedside table is a little light bedtime reading. A discourse on the symbolism of a single painting by Van Eyck, for example. Another on the history of the color black. A book of Elizabethan poetry. The latest translation of Aristotle.

A study of public toilets.

I do not share or fully understand Herb's passions…or his affinity for clutter. But he understands me. When I seem irritable, he hustles to clean up his mushrooming piles of paper. When I question myself, he reassures me. And when I am blue, he comforts me. "I think you need a hug," he says. Or "How about a cup of tea and a little massage?"

Unlike mine, Herb's internal barometer is almost always set to fair and calm. He needs very little and asks for even less. Whatever I offer or give, he appreciates; what I don't, he accepts. He does not begrudge me my late, slow awakenings and solitary mornings or my time away with family or friends. He is content standing and reading in the living room, tinkering in his basement carpentry workshop, trying out new recipes in the kitchen. When I return, wherever he may be, he greets me with a childlike delight.

One evening, Herb accompanies me to a class in guided meditation. He does not need it; I do. Despite his modeling, I am a tangle of regrets and worries, should-haves and to-dos. I need to find my center.

The leader asks us to close our eyes and visualize a place we have felt completely at peace. I quickly settle on the memory of lying next to Herb in bed, my head on his chest, his arms embracing me, in the afterglow of sex. My eyes still closed, I smile privately, then inhale and exhale slowly, as the teacher instructs. I am transported to Nirvana. I am bliss incarnate.

Afterwards, the leader asks for volunteers to share the places they envisioned. One woman says, "I imagined the beach where my family vacationed when I was young. The whoosh of the waves rolling in on the sand." Another talks about her grandmother's lakeside cottage, and still another, a brook. Everyone, it seems, has been meditating to a G-rated image of a childhood summer by water's edge.

I do not raise my hand. Neither does Herb. I wonder about that. Is he just being circumspect, as usual? Or was he, too, picturing the two of us entwined?

I pose the question when we are alone, heading to our car. "So what were you visualizing?" I ask.

Herb stops walking and turns to me. Slowly, a smile spreads across his face. "The reading room of the British Museum," he says dreamily.

My heart sinks. We walk the rest of the way in silence.

"Why? What about you?" he asks after he begins driving.

"I don't want to tell you," I answer.

"Okay," he says. He's like that—respectful. But I know he can feel me stewing.

"You can tell me," he says.

"No, it's embarrassing," I say. "Pathetic, even."

"I doubt that," he says. He pulls into our driveway, opens the door to our house.

"So?" he asks as we walk inside.

I spill it out. Herb laughs. Not at me, it is clear: at the disconnect, and mostly at himself. He doesn't think I'm pathetic at all; he feels bad for hurting my feelings. He wonders if this latest gaffe has confirmed his fear, or mine, that he is a secret Vulcan, only posing as a human being.

"I'm never going to live this down, am I?" he asks.

"No," I admit. And then I laugh too.

It is five years later now and we are still laughing. My husband's home is in a reading room, inside the pages of a book.

My home is with him.

BABA'S SUMMER

Louisa Howerow

More than 117,000 are displaced inside Ukraine, 87% of them from the Donetsk and Luhansk regions. Source: 2014 UN refugee agency.

My father leans against the windowsill,
staring at leafless poplars pinned against
sunlit blue. I remind him that Anna, his aide,
is waiting to help him into the shower. "Anna,"

he gives the name a Slavic tilt, even though
she's told him her mother picked the name
from a movie whose title she's forgotten.
Anna will rinse away rankness, incontinence.

She'll hum and call him love. Rub him down
and sooth his thin skin with lotions before
wrapping him warm. Anna moves near him,
takes his elbow. "Indian summer,
good day for a walk." "No," he says.
"We call it Baba's summer."
Through the open bathroom door
his hoarse, breathy voice is reminding Anna

not to trap toads, while I wonder and hope
he remembers what I remember:

me, at eight, under a yellowing poplar
holding a warty toad
he won't let me keep.

Midges rise,
a frenzied twirling above uncut grass.
Baba's summer, I hear again, and he's trailed off
into a Ukrainian village, his dream of return.
Not worth telling him Luhansk is unrecognizable.

WHEN ASKED ABOUT MY SISTER'S TRAU-

RK Taylor

my father responds that 52% of marriages
end, that millions of children are well-adjusted
post-divorce. i want to ask:

how many children have dialed
9-1-1 when hearing their mother scream
in a wendy's parking lot
years after the divorce?
or locked themselves in a bedroom
in their own home
after the walls
have been fist-marred?
what percentage of elementary-aged kids
have watched their mother
apply makeup on a monday morning—
covering burns and bruises with blush?

APPLE

Gay Baines

Yesterday I cut an apple not
stem to blackened sepal, the
usual way, but crossways, so I could
see the ghost of blossom petals
in the creamy flesh. I do this
during the plains of February—
to acknowledge spring, even as
other people (not I) put aside
the sweetness of apple and pear,
papaya and prune—for the stark
black bread of Lent. I know their
rejoicing will be dampened by
over-excitement and chocolate
as mine will be sweetened for
letting flesh be flesh, and life
be life, even if not blessed.

THEOLDWHITEHOUSE
Stephan Campbell
Medium: Digital

HARDWOOD FLOOR

Christopher Woods

My dead grandmother
Was carried out of the house
But the wood still sang.

When Vietnam called
My soldier brother
Hesitated before going,
Found time to
Push me down the stairs,
Try to strangle me
Because I was reading
Books by Chairman Mao.
The floor remembers.

Later when my father lay dying
In celebration and in dirge,
A family possibly ending,
The floor knew and guided us.

This is how a house lives
Beyond namesake or the people
Who wander its spine.
This is how wood lives,
Remembering the forest,

A step here and there,
Across a floor,
In a clearing.

SMILES IN THE FOG

Kristin Bryant Rajan

It starts with the little things,
unimportant matters,
debris cluttering the brain:
When to prune the hydrangeas?
How many cups of flour in the sugar cookies?

"I always forget,"
she says smiling.
"When did you say you're coming to visit?
Is it this week or next?"

We repeat and repeat,
stifling the urge to exclaim
"I already told you that!"—
exasperation more fear
than anger.

When it's just the two of us,
my brother and I,
with furrowed concentration,
we try to remember ourselves
what it is we said,
what it is she forgot.
Amused

somewhat
that we can't recall
what our mother can't remember.

She too laughs,
"You know my memory,"
she says with the smile
of one who doesn't truly know
her memory.
Because if she did,
she wouldn't smile.

But we all smile.

Fog and smiles abound,
nobody knows for sure
what's been said,
what's been forgotten.

The doctor asks her to remember five words:
cake, rainbow, money, book, purple.
With the pride of an elementary spelling bee champ,
she recites them immediately through a victorious smile.

But after a conversation of
cholesterol and exercise,
blood pressure and sleep habits,
she can't remember one
of those five words.

"Were there five?"

Too random, we say;
no connection, we justify;
you remember what's important
we lie.

But is this how it happens?
First the random words go,
then the dates for pruning,
the measurements in recipes.

There are levels of small:
birthdays, graduations,
the ages of the grandkids:
"They're not both in high school are they?!"

And even that makes sense,
can be justified,
time ebbing and flowing
then cascading—
motions of moments always fleeting fast.

Hard to understand
how infants
become teenagers;
how children
become middle aged adults
trying hard to remember
what is it their mother has forgotten.

SUNDAYS AND SHADOWS

Kristin Bryant Rajan

My father met a woman
where the waves break on the shore
at our family cookout on the beach.
He followed salt crystal prisms in her hair
deep into the sand dunes
where sedge grass hid them from sun and eyes.
They stayed until the sand no longer held the warmth of day.

My aunt and uncle took me home that Sunday night.

Even now, decades from that age of twelve,
charcoal and pot still smell the same to me.
The smoke of family cookouts and marijuana intermingle in my mind,
musky air to whet the appetite
for women who might pass by,
brittle patterns of hamburgers left too long on the grill.

I don't remember many conversations
we had on Sundays,
our day together.
Through the smoke,
his face was heavy,
silent as stone.
Deadened by defeat:

a failed marriage,
a hated job,
a distant daughter.
Sometimes he smiled,
particularly when a pretty girl was near,
but that was rare.
It was often just the two of us.

When there was a girlfriend in his life,
his face awakened.
He'd make jokes and buy me ice cream cones.
A new name interwoven in our dialogue;
a new perfume cloyed to the vinyl seats of his Datsun B210.
Then that one would disappear
and so would the ice cream,
and so would the smiles.

I tried to fill the silence
with the only small talk
one so small can find.

On Sundays,
my father lying on the couch
staring at an open window.
I would lean over him,
strain to see what it was he saw.
But he wasn't looking at the trees
or the shapes their shadows made on sidewalks.
He didn't see me seeing him,
bending my body in ways that hurt

to try to find his vantage point.
His vision clouded by his misery.

Sundays always ended with the sunset;
that's when he took me home.

I tried to make Sundays
feel like fun,
or look like fun.
I wanted to bring Sunday's light
inside my father's studio apartment.

But he was stuck inside the shadows,
and I was too small to pull him out.

WEEDING AROUND CARROTS IN MY MOTHER'S GARDEN

Joette Varnado

2009

Kneeling next to my mother in her garden,
our knees wrist-deep in rich manure,
flexible bone and blood writhing with worms.
One by one, we pluck weeds like feathers
from loose chicken skin. I wiggle a daisy-gloved finger
into the dirt; feeling for an orange scalp
before ripping the weed with a deep,
whispery *thump*! Beside me, my mother dangles
each one in front of her face, evaluates its hairiness,
shaking the clumps of dirt that cling
between the fibers. Sometimes she'll give
a satisfactory grunt to the ones she had caught
before they could close their tendrils
around a young carrot root in a tight
headlock. The only other sound slicing
through the rhythm of our weed-pulling
is the high-pitched whine from the dog
behind us; the scruff of her neck clutched
in my father's fist shoving her head down, burying
her snout in the loose dirt surrounding a small,
shallow hole she dug on the other side
of my mother's garden. I steal a glance at my mother

flinging the long, green stalks onto a growing heap
without turning her head, without saying a word.
Tomorrow, I will eat her steamed carrots until my plate
is empty. And the hole I see outside through the window
will slowly mud and pool with rainwater.

MY AMERICAN STAR QUILT

Mary Louise Kiernan

somewhere in the unknown world/a yellow eyed woman/
sits with her daughter/quilting. ~ Lucille Clifton

my star quilt   outstretched across my car's hood
another   yard sale   another   letting go
another home to pack up   releasing   once again
when a young mother with two little ones claims
her church is collecting blankets   for victims
of Hurricane Katrina   in New Orleans, Louisiana

I'd handsewn bias tape   to make loops to hang it
too perfect, too precious   to use as a blanket
I think back   to the summer day   I first held it
a hundred dollars saved to buy post-baby clothes
instead I turned back   to the upscale shop
in Bridgehampton   east of the Indian reservation

Stitched by   Native American tribeswomen
a platinumed saleswoman   took pride in telling
wrapping it   in layers   of aqua tissue paper
as if it might break   Yes, please take it, I say
to the young mother   a yellow eyed woman
teaching me   my quilt was never mine   to keep

WHAT SHE FRACTURED

Karen George

It began with a plastic-framed handheld mirror, minutes after Skye returned home from her husband's funeral. At fifty-five, Evan had not survived a heart attack. *Myocardial infarction, coronary thrombosis* — words the emergency room doctor gave her.

His coworker, Colin, wouldn't stop telling her the details at the funeral home layout. *Layout* — a horrible term. Everything and everyone on display — *laid out*. Colin went on and on about how, in their company cafeteria, talking, laughing about Trump's latest debacle, Evan had measured off a spoonful of key lime pie, and raised it to his mouth. How his arm fell to the table, the spoon clanged and spun. How he slumped sideways in his chair and slid to the floor. A woman screamed. Colin tried to straighten him out, listen for a heartbeat. "But he was gone."

Colin had already told her these details of Evan's last few moments alive, when he met her at the hospital. Now, at the funeral home, he zeroed in on the key lime pie, and how much her husband loved key lime pie, as if she didn't know Evan's preferences. She supposed Colin was as nervous as she was, talking to fill the space.

The intense scent of roses and lilies overwhelmed the room. Her arm, her hand tingled. She might slap Colin if he mentioned key lime pie one more time. Her mouth assumed the bittersweet, sour taste of that damned pie, which she hated and her husband loved. Skye needed silence, she kept thinking, space to breathe, to listen, to wait for what came next, and to see if time enfolded her.

She stood beside the open casket, accepted hugs from people as they streamed past for the viewing. Another barbaric practice, in her opinion. She tried not to look at Evan. Peripherally she glimpsed his pale gray shirt, and his tie striped lavender, mulberry and silver. If only he'd open his lids once more, so she could memorize his eyes — dusky umber.

"Yes, he was sure enjoying that key lime pie," she heard Colin say, a few feet away. "He closed his eyes, as if to taste it better."

She focused on breathing to stop the shivers in her belly. Yes, Evan had a habit of savoring things with his eyes closed, especially when he sipped a good, dry wine, as they had the night before he died. Four days ago.

They'd turned off MSNBC on the T.V., nauseated by replays of Trump bragging, and repeating *no collusion* three times, like some goddamned charm, in a rant that neither made sense nor resembled a sentence.

"Alexa," Evan had instructed the voice assistant device, "Please play Norah Jones' *Come Away with Me* album on low volume."

Pillows behind their backs at either ends of the couch, ankles touching, they held glasses of Malbec. Opening chords of "Don't Know Why" sounded, followed by the singer's breathy voice. A platter of spreadable gorgonzola and one-inch squares of extra-sharp cheddar lay on the cocktail table within reach. Evan pushed his soles against hers, trying to instigate a foot wrestle.

"Don't make me spill any of this." She luxuriated in the wine's smoky flavor and aroma that suggested dark fruits.

Evan popped a cheddar square into his mouth, and sipped some wine. He closed his eyes, hummed the song's refrain. After a few minutes of silence, he inhaled deeply, and opened his warm brown eyes. "What if we quit our jobs, sold everything, and moved to Europe?"

She shouldn't have been surprised. He watched every episode of HGTV's House Hunters International, taking notes and updating a spreadsheet on the most reasonable places to live abroad.

"I've narrowed it down to Prague; Budapest; Oporto, Portugal; Riga, Latvia; Rijeka, Croatia."

A pain, like panic, like exhilaration, surged in her as her husband slowly enunciated the litany of names, as if each held a particular flavor.

"Ljubljana, Slovenia; Tallinn, Estonia; Saint-Chinian, France; Abruzzi, Italy."

Skye gave no reply. Slid her lids closed. Wandered villages alongside vineyards, the mountains, the sea. *Maybe.*

Skye had raced home from Evan's funeral, everything she'd repressed gagging her. Well-meaning friends and family had whispered she had to *get a hold of herself* when she'd begun full-body weeping and shaking. They feared she wouldn't be able to get through the day. It took her breath away — others telling her how to behave at her husband's funeral. But fury had allowed her to cork the grief for the moment, prevent the consummate weight of her loss to smother her.

As she drove home at dangerous speeds, she disgorged scream after scream, mouth stretched wide open as if to empty herself. She turned onto her street lined with goddamned gorgeous pears, cherries, and magnolias flowering. Their beauty stabbed her.

She retched when she reached their master bathroom. The sour-sweet stench choked her, buckled her legs. She leaned on the vanity counter, opened the drawer that held fresh washcloths, wanting something cold on her face. A folded square of paper lay atop the sea-green cotton. A chill prickled her arms.

Let's do it! A squiggly *"E,"* Evan's signature. One of his endearing habits, leaving her notes tucked here and there.

Skye grabbed the puke-pink handle of a mirror, lifted it from the counter. She wanted to smash it into the wall mirror before her, entrapping all of her but her legs. Her dark purple dress suggested something raw and slithery broken loose. Her fist tightened around the handle. A salty, metallic taste bloomed on her tongue.

Raising her arm high, she slammed the handheld mirror into the sink. Shards skittered everywhere. Slivers hit her face—one below an eye, one on her cheek near her ear.

"My god, I could have put out an eye."

Her instinct was to grab the mirror to check close-up for a piece embedded in her face. She flung the mirror's empty frame into the garbage can, stared at the array of what looked like stars against the pearl-gray bowl of the sink. Relief washed through her, strong as a sexual release.

"Look at the fucking mess you made."

Skye leaned toward the wall mirror, knocking fragments off the vanity top. Remembering a mirror in her purse, she moved toward the living room. Her heels crunched bits against the tile floor, dragged sharp particles onto the carpet. It took an hour to clean up the debris, a slow and methodical process. A calmness, a euphoria settled around her like a tub of hot bathwater.

All night she dreamt of that mirror, crashing it again and again into the milky gray bowl of the sink that morphed into the plush black urn of night sky. Star specks flashed a message she struggled to decode. She lowered a large chunk of glass to her wrist, poised to tear herself open. Woke with a giddy panic swirling inside her, itching to throw something, to watch it shatter.

In the dining room her eyes fell on the hutch, plates tilted for optimal viewing. Goosebumps rose on her arms. She removed a plate from its niche. She barely remembered the person she had been thirty years ago when they chose the Vintage Tuscan England bone china collection for their wedding registry. As if all her later selves overlaid her young self, a kind of firing process similar to the glaze firing used in the making of bone china.

They rarely used it anymore. She stared at the pattern she had once loved. On a luminous white background, a black vine with lacy leaves cascaded along the rim. Poppies of bright aqua, rose-pink, and yellow with chartreuse tiny leaves. *Bone china,* stamped on the back. So beautiful and volatile her wrists ached, making her think of broken bones. The skeletal system — too many crackable parts.

Bone china, clay mixed with bone ash—crushed cattle bones, milled into fine particles. It sickened her when she read about the ash of cow bones contained in her china. She'd thought *bone* referred to its white color.

In the kitchen, she balanced the plate in the palm of her hand. So light, so fragile. How upset she was when she broke one of the saucers a few years into their marriage. She'd planned to see if a replacement could be ordered, but never did.

Unease paired with buoyancy in her midriff. When she pulled open the basement door a cool breeze almost made her drop the plate. She stepped down onto the landing, clutched the railing with one hand.

The funeral director had led Skye to the casket for a final viewing. She couldn't tell the man she did not want to see Evan that way. She'd concentrated on his silk tie, immersed herself in its lavender, mulberry, silver.

She flung the plate down the stairs. It splintered with a burst eerie as a high-pitched screech — a vibration in her throat. A thin dust rose. Or did she imagine it? She thought again of those cows and the ash of their bones. Her arm and shoulder radiated warmth. It didn't make sense, she knew, pulverizing objects she once cherished. Keepsakes.

She wandered room to room, sweating, weeping, desperate to slam one of the delicate teacups. A pile of empty boxes her sister Myra had dropped off lay by the front door. The dining room table held sympathy cards; a book listing names of all who attended the funeral service; planters and vases of flowers sent by co-workers, neighbors, family and friends.

From a small box, Skye picked up a leftover holy card. The Blessed Virgin Mary silhouetted from the waist up, in a sea of incandescent white lilies. She cradled the baby Jesus. Behind them, a dark sky of splintery stars. On the back, the *Memorare* prayer. Skye recalled her mother reciting those words twice daily for a month—a novena for special intentions, such as when her aunt was diagnosed with breast cancer, or Skye's father with throat cancer. How desperately her mother prayed, believing with all her heart that Mary would intercede to save them.

Skye consumed much of the next two weeks with shattering and sweeping up the remains. She broke the vases and ceramic pots people sent to express their sympathy, and stuffed the plants and flowers into the garbage can. Then she returned to her fine bone china, only allowing herself to break one piece a day. With each plate, saucer, bowl or cup, she shunned lumps of herself.

Sometimes she cried while she cleared away the breakage. But she could not deny how much calmer she felt afterwards, how gratifying she found smashing anything too painful to see. Her wreckage remained a secret. On the basement stair landing she kept heavy leather boots. On a hook, safety goggles. Overkill, because she threw from near the top of the stairs. If she ventured down a few steps, she gripped the railing with one hand while she hurled with the other.

She thought of her demolition as blood-letting, *phlebotomy,* the medieval practice of draining blood to cure illnesses. She didn't want to hurt herself, or she might have turned to cutting. She'd been tempted that first time, staring at the sharp dregs of mirror she'd broken after the funeral. It would have been so easy to choose a larger chunk, to slit her wrist a little.

It scared her how addictive breaking became, but she was careful. When she returned to work, she limited herself to just one binge a day, then one a week at the year anniversary of Evan's death. She settled into her new life as a single woman, met friends for dinner, a movie, play, or concert. She never invited anyone to her house. No one questioned why.

On the second anniversary of Evan's death, Skye decided on saving money to fulfill her husband's proposal of moving to Europe. Sure, it hadn't been her dream, but she accepted it as something she wanted to try for herself — a different kind of breaking. She needed to select a destination. What about Asia or South America? She started watching *House Hunters International,* and updating Evan's spreadsheet.

Her father had worked for a national law firm that required the family move every few years, so Skye and Myra grew accustomed to leaving friends and making new ones. Upheaval felt normal. Skye had no children. Her only sibling, Myra, had raised her son Orin alone, would never reveal who his father was, at least not to Skye. A year ago, Orin died in a Tennessee wildfire, on vacation with his fiancé. They attempted to outrun the flames. Their truck hurtled over an embankment, their bodies found a hundred feet away. Six months later, Myra married a rich man ten years younger than her. He spoiled her any way she'd let him.

Skye kept two plates of her china intact. The rest she broke, feeling lighter, stronger with each item flung. Her sense of wellbeing and control increased with each release executed. She grew enchanted, obsessed with the sound of delicate china striking the basement floor — intricate as tiny bells or wind chimes, the way it echoed off the cement floor and walls. Every object had its own notes disintegrating — a saucer different than a dinner plate or teacup. She supposed it had to do with weight.

She didn't always clean the broken slivers up right away. She'd waited a month or two before donning thick leather work gloves and boots to sweep the residue into a dustpan, dump it into black heavy-duty, tripled garbage bags, roll the can to the curb. She didn't want anyone to get cut.

Once she'd shattered all their fine bone china except for two plates, she switched to their crystal stemware. Before dropping each piece, she turned them to refract light off their diamond-cut pattern, and extended her arm as if offering Chardonnay to a guest. She set aside two wine glasses, the ones she and Evan had used the night before he died. They'd joked that wine tasted better out of shimmery, expensive crystal. Neither of them knew or cared about the difference between wine goblets: sherry, margarita, or martini glasses, and champagne flutes.

How little all that mattered. Yes, how fun, to choose and register for all the beautiful fine china and crystal stemware. She'd felt luxurious and sophisticated. But the fun they enjoyed together, their adventures as Evan called them, remained the real keepsakes: climbing Machu Picchu, hiking in the Grand Canyon (they had the knees to prove it), parasailing in Key West, and white water rafting in a glacial river in Iceland. Evan had even convinced her to zipline in Jaguar Cove, Belize and Costa Rica's Monteverde Cloud Forest Reserve.

When no crystal stemware remained, except for two wine glasses, Skye visited thrift stores, flea markets, and antique malls, looking for chipped china that cost next to nothing. She'd get panicked if she didn't have a surplus of items ready to ruin.

The sound of severing became a kind of music. The finest porcelain clinked, reminiscent of the piercing ring at the far right end of a piano keyboard. If no fine china was available, she hurled heavy stoneware that cracked apart in bigger chunks—a jarring clatter that resembled the abysmal piano keys on the far left. Instead of slamming an object at the floor, sometimes she arced one for the closest basement wall, like a Frisbee. That tone varied slightly from that of concussing the floor. Other times she let a piece slip softly from her hand. But she could not bear to miss its descent, its moment of impact. This notion of anticipating, and participating as witness to the fall, got her musing about the dynamics of falling, and what it felt like to plummet.

One day in her third year of ruin, she bought a Homer Laughlin bluebird plate so exquisite she yearned to keep it for herself — beauty to contemplate when she didn't want to go to work, or when an anniversary caught her off-guard. Three bluebirds viewed from above, wings extended, with the edges of soft pink underbellies visible, matching pink flowers attached to a vine-like stem linking the three together.

Painted mid-flight, the birds reminded her of the out-of-control tingle of ziplining high above ground, knowing she'd fracture so many bones if she fell. An ache seethed in her, so strong, she feared she might be having a heart attack. She forced herself to send the plate flying, imagined the birds finally set free to ascend into blue, blue sky.

She hadn't purged the remains in a while. Quite a pile had accumulated. She enjoyed stepping on the pieces as she swept. Cracking the already broken created its own unique jangle. Her sweeping raised a powdery film, released a scent redolent of chalk. She wondered if dust contained in particles of cement jarred loose when struck.

As she gathered chips in a dustpan, she remembered the NPR interview about people jumping off the Golden Gate Bridge. They'd talked to an actual survivor. Skye had pulled off the highway, overcome with relief that she never decided to jump off anything. The thought of her bones cracking terrified her. Still, she speculated about leaping — the interval before rupture. What if she'd stepped off a tall building? A bridge or canyon? What sound would her body make breaking?

Skye rolled the carry-on suitcase to her front door. It held the only things she owned now. Her steps echoed, the house emptied of furniture and carpets. When she completed one last task, she'd call a cab to take her to the airport.

She'd sold her house, car, and wall art. The rest she'd donated to Habitat for Humanity and veterans organizations. She'd quit her job, transferred money abroad. Said goodbye to friends, her sister and brother-in-law. A few promised to visit. Skye refused several offers to accompany her to search for an apartment to rent. She assured them the realtor she'd contacted could handle it.

She'd decided on Prague. To stay a year or two, then maybe move to Budapest or Reykjavik, Iceland.

Skye lifted two plates and two wine glasses from the floor—the remaining physical symbols of her marriage—and headed for the basement. When she opened the door, a sweet powdery aroma met her, especially strong from her intensive sweeping a few hours ago. Now, to compose one last mess.

She set the plates and glasses on the landing. What happiness all those years ago when she and Evan picked out wedding registry items at McAlpin's Department Store — the moment of bliss when her eyes found the intricate pattern she chose to begin their life together.

In each palm she balanced a twin plate. Her gaze followed its lime green leaves, the poppies lemon yellow, magenta, and robin's egg blue. Hugging the curve of the plate's rim, an arched branch reached inky black into bone-white sky. She pressed her lips against its tiny eye-shaped leaves.

She clanged both plates together like cymbals before dropping them. Her fingers vibrated. One plate landed a second before the other in an exquisite burst that echoed through the empty chamber. A gauzy haze rose — a reversal, she mused — a release back to their bone ash.

She cradled the crystal bowl of each wine goblet. The diamond-etched pattern tickled her skin. She closed her eyes, slipped back to the last night of her husband's life, when they held these glasses filled with Malbec. How Evan opened his eyes, pecan brown. Posed the idea of moving to Europe. An odd mix of alarm and arousal flooded her.

She breathed deeply. The musty smell of the basement reminded her of the pungent cheese they'd nibbled — gorgonzola, extra sharp cheddar. She'd been asleep when he left for work the following morning. When she'd entered the kitchen, the crystal wine glasses lay upside down in the sink. She'd washed them, the fragrance of dish soap fusing with the wine's tang.

Her eyes opened, and she clinked the goblets together, raised them as in a toast. Their shape suggested Catholic chalices believed to hold the symbolic body and blood of Christ.

"Evan," she whispered, before hurling the vessel at the basement wall. The crash sent shivers up her arms. Shards skittered against the floor like the tinkle of a charm bracelet. She imagined Evan preceding her to Prague. She flung the last glass. Breaking herself open one last time.

LOMONTVILLE, NEW YORK

Matthew J. Spireng

If I go out in the tilled fields
near my home, some places
stone tools thousands of years old
are more plentiful than the geese

that pass through in the fall:
projectile points, knives, scrapers,
drills chipped of chert by men
who never wrote. Celts, adzes,

gouges shaped and smoothed
so they still shine despite the
long passage of time. If I
look around at my neighbors

there is no trace of those men who
came before, none whatsoever. We
have taken over and they are gone.
But what, I wonder, is there that I have

made with my hands that will survive

as long as their work? If some man
goes out in these fields thousands of years
from now, won't it still be their tools he finds?

PENNSYLVANIA QUILT

Kezia Kynaston-Mitchell

one cool gray day we drove out to the mountain;
smell of damp earth and the turning leaves
and you counted out the places you'd lived
taking me on a tour of your past:
the farms, the weatherboard houses leaning with age,
lurching from a different time,
and light fog skimmed the corn.

with you, watching the trees set fire to the fall,
mapping your three lives from valley to summit
and seeing the places from your stories
—where grant broke his leg, the cliff you rode bikes off,
the place the first butch girl you loved lived—
i discovered america.

i had circumnavigated without circumspection
came three thousand miles to meet you;
i was columbus without the genocide and horrific diaries,
patching together a new world
that belonged to someone else.

the parks, the museum, the new favorite artists;
the wonderfully worn fifties fixtures at the drive-in
where we watched horror movies, drank coke in the rain;

kissing you in a tree house, getting playfully
heckled by new yorkers on the hiking trails;

gas station snacks, *Gettysburg to Glory* back-to-back,
pecking two hundred years from your mother's pocket:
italy, slovenia, ukraine alongside the carolinas,
the bodies traded as property, whose names
you'll never know. we wore our volunteering
as if it wasn't a dream for our future, petted
shelter cats and pitbulls, dropped hopes into collection
boxes while the chamber music played.

we ate pizza for days and skulked by your old schools
from preparatory to textile-mill-husk, patterned the
change from hall of learning to prison-flavored
warehouse, where your second minority
was in not going to juvie. you are truly the changeling
rainbow, with your double-barreled lifetimes
and your mind so wide you can see both sides of any
argument and bend them to meet in the middle.
you were the most equanimous patriot
until bipartisanship splintered your spirit.

we passed old marquee signs and convents
rising like crumbled wings, peeked through the trees
to glimpse the things you'd seen with other eyes,
and
then
along the roads we played a form of bingo
with the bumper stickers and ugly campaign signs.

twenty points per confederate flag
seen on the back of a truck in a northern state,
and i didn't believe "aryan princess" was a thing
until i saw decals in glittery pink font:
some blonde with acrylic tips and perpetual
beige-lipped sneer, clutching the wheel
like it was the last great white hope.

you explained to me how to spot
the girls wearing more than i earn in a year
as we wondered whether deprivation
was truly to blame for intolerance;
i saw my first redneck in camo, grunting
his disapproval at us in the grocery store line

and some guy in the parking lot shook his head in disbelief
as he took your picture from inside his truck.
perhaps we are somebody's outraged facebook share,
the symbol of everything wrong with his country
—you know, the mirror-world one where masses never huddled
and nothing was built on a sinking foundation of bloody flesh
and the city on the hill isn't tarnished—
because you have a pride flag patch on the tactical hat
you wear to the range, and your wet-down curls and slender waist
seem to confuse the coal crackers as well as outrage
the skinhead white nationalist scum of the keystone state.

i've told you a dozen times that you shouldn't be ashamed;
we both know better than to think that this country
is defined by its weakness. a quilt holds the world inside
its kaleidoscope scraps, makes cast-offs into jewels,

and if torn is never sundered but just sewn again,
a square upon square pieced in time,
a warmth stronger for being the sum
of its parts, its fabrics and stitches.

CONTRIBUTORS

Gay Baines is a member of the Roycroft Wordsmiths. She has a B.A. in English from Russell Sage College and has done graduate work at Syracuse University and SUNY - Buffalo. Her poem "Cicadas" has been nominated for Sundress Publications' 2019 Best of the Net Anthology.

Soares Braga is a 33-year-old Portuguese writing enthusiast. He holds a degree in archaeology by the University of Lisbon. Currently, Braga is working as a transcriber and pursuing a master's degree in history and culture of religions. He worked and volunteered in the areas of education, culture, sciences, and politics.

Stephan Campbell (b. Kansas City, Missouri) moved to California with the rest of the "Art Okies" of the 60's and 70's. Writing for local rags and art-zines, Campbell, also a visual artist, was a finalist in several digital art competitions, including 1st place entries in Macworld and other.

Joseph Crossley is a writer of short fiction and poetry. He was born in 2000 in Leamington Spa. He is a regular contributor at the Friday Flash Fiction blog.

Steven Dale Davison has published poems in a number of journals. He also has written both short and long fiction, plays in both verse and produced, some of them produced, and published essays and nonfiction book chapters. Mr. Davison has worked as a journalist and writer in the private sector.

Meredith Field is a self-taught artist of 10 years. After high school she realized that her passion was entertainment and decided to further her career with a college education. She strives to become a lead designer for Sony Entertainment upon completion of her bachelor's in multi-media.

Harvey Flowers mimics biological forms and reconstructs the way people look at nature by creating organic shapes that imitate natural objects. He primarily work in clay but also tries to merge multiple mediums together to create more complex structures. Harvey takes inspiration from nature and biology. Some of his inspirations are derived from his scientific background in anatomy, zoology, botany, microbiology, ecology and geology. He prefers the use of recycled materials or to use ecologically friendly methods when creating. He would like for people to consider their impact on the environment. While he prefers three-dimensional work, He also has an interest in photography and printmaking, and tends to use a lot of the same imagery only on a two-dimensional plane.

Karen George is author of five chapbooks, and two poetry collections from Dos Madres Press: Swim Your Way Back and A Map and One Year. She reviews poetry at http://readwritepoetry.blogspot.com/ and is fiction editor of the online journal Waypoints: http://www.waypointsmag.com/. Her website is: https://karenlgeorge.blogspot.com/.

Elaine Guo was born in Zhengzhou, China, and has lived in Vancouver, New York, and Southern California. She recently graduated from Claremont McKenna College with degrees in History and International Relations, and plans to continue graduate studies in Medieval Chinese history in the United Kingdom. She has loved stories and books since before she could read, and is currently working on a novel set in 18th century London.

jd hegarty is a lawyer, a poet, and an essayist living in Saint Paul, Minnesota with two loud grey cats. They have an MFA from Hamline University. jd's work can be found in Chronotope, White Stag, Crab Orchard Review, and Mortar Magazine. Their first chapbook, On Passing was published by Red Bird Chapbooks in 2017. They can be reached at jdhegarty.com.

Louisa Howerow's poems have appeared in a number of anthologies, among them: Gush: Menstrual Manifestos for Our Times (Frontenac House), Another Dysfunctional Cancer Poem Anthology (Mansfield Press), River of Earth and Sky: Poems for the Twenty-First Century (1st World Publishing), and I Found It at the Movies: An Anthology of Film Poems (Guernica).

Mary Louise Kiernan's poems have been published in The Delmarva Review, Pudding Magazine, Hudson Valley Echoes, Chronogram, ArtSpace, Common Ground Review, Broad River Review, and the "Metropolitan Diary" in The New York Times. In 2015 she was awarded the Adult Poetry Prize by Tempe Public Library and Arizona State University.

Stephen Linsteadt is an artist, writer, and poet. His work is an ongoing exploration into the study of cosmology, alchemy, and the archetypal symbolism of Carl Jung. He is a published poet and the author of "The Heart of the Hero" and the poetry collection "The Beauty of Curved Space."

Lennart Lundh is a poet, short-fictionist, historian, and photographer. His work has appeared internationally since 1965.

W. Joseph Lutz started writing when he was in college, then stopped for a few decades, and only recently has started writing again. He is a member of the Wisconsin Fellowship of Poets and also enjoys acting on stage.

DS Maolalai has been nominated three times for Best of the Net and twice for the Pushcart Prize. His poetry has been released in two collections, Love is Breaking Plates in the Garden (Encircle Press) and Sad Havoc Among the Birds (Turas Press).

Joanne Nelson's writing appears in a variety of anthologies and literary journals and her work has aired on WUWM, her local NPR affiliate. Nelson lives in Hartland, Wisconsin where she develops and leads community programs, maintains a psychotherapy practice, and adjuncts. More information is available at wakeupthewriterwithin.com.

Joette Varnado is currently earning her MFA at Southern Illinois University, Carbondale. A native of Houston, Texas, she holds a Bachelor of Fine Arts degree from Stephen F. Austin State University. She has several publications from SFASU's Literary Journal, as well as The Rappahannock Review, The Midwest Quarterly, The Writing Cooperative, The Noteworthy Journal, and more. Lauren is also a virtual assistant for hire who offers graphic design, freelance writing, and blogging services to brands and businesses. For more work, please visit www.laurenmichelemcdaniel.com and follow her @LaurenMcDaniel4 on Twitter.

Kezia Kynaston-Mitchell is a transatlantic poet, author, and artist, splitting their time between southwest England and northeast Pennsylvania. Perpetually somewhere between forests and rocky beaches, yet steadfastly unable to surf, Kezia enjoys hiking and B-movie appreciation, and is a passionate animal welfare advocate and canine fosterer. @KeziaKynaston for Twitter and www.keziakynastonmitchell.com for website contact.

Trevor Oattes is a Canadian writer of horror and fantasy. His short horror stories are set within the quiet isolation of Canadian winter, where evil things hide just beyond the snowfall. Oattes makes his living as a reporter and has been published in newspapers and magazines throughout Canada.

Lauro Palomba has taught ESL and done stints as a freelance journalist and speechwriter. Approximately eighty of his poems and stories have appeared in American and Canadian literary journals.

Dvora Wolff Rabino received her BA in journalism and mass communications from NYU and her JD from Columbia University. Previous essays and stories of Dvora's have been published – many under the pen name of Ariella Neulander – in Linden Avenue Literary Journal, Penmen Review, Santa Fe Writers Project, and Steam Ticket.

Kristin Bryant Rajan writes poetry, fiction, creative nonfiction, and literary criticism in Atlanta. She is widely published in literary/creative writing journals as well as anthologies and is a Pushcart and Best of the Net nominee. She teaches English at Kennesaw State University, facilitates happiness workshops, and teaches spin classes.

Ellie Roscher is the author of Play Like a Girl, How Coffee Saved my Life and 12 Tiny Things (forthcoming). She holds an MFA from Sarah Lawrence in Creative Nonfiction Writing and an MA in Theology from Luther Seminary. She lives in Minneapolis with her spouse and two sons.

Erica Schimmel is currently earning a master's degree in library science to complement her master's degree in children's literature. When she isn't working in her library, she is hiking in the mountains, reading, or making art.

Fariel Shafee has degrees in science, but enjoys writing and art. She has exhibited both digital art and paintings internationally.

Geo. Staley is retired from teaching at Portland Community College. His poetry has appeared in Chest, Four Quarters, Loonfeather, New Mexico Humanities Review, Fireweed, Freshwater, Santa Fe Literary Review, and others. He has a short story in a recent issue of Plainsong.

Gregor Southard was born and raised in Topeka, Kansas. After graduating from the University of Kansas with a BA in theatre and film, he moved to Nashville to pursue a career in entertainment production. He eventually landed a management position at the Ryman Auditorium.

Matthew J. Spireng's books are What Focus Is from Word Press and Out of Body (Bluestem Press), winner of the 2004 Bluestem Poetry Award at Emporia State University, and the chapbooks Clear Cut, Young Farmer (Finishing Line Press), Encounters (Finishing Line Press), Inspiration Point (Bright Hill Press), and Just This. He is an eight-time Pushcart Prize nominee.

RK Taylor earned his MFA in Pittsburgh from Chatham University. A Pushcart and PEN/Dau nominee, Taylor had work featured in Scribble, Origami Poems Project, Flash Fiction Magazine, among others. He has worked with homeless families, children with autism, and inmates at the Allegheny County Jail. To find out more, visit www.writerRKTaylor.com.

Cynthia Trenshaw served as hospital chaplain, midwife to the dying, and street massage therapist to homeless people. Meeting in the Margins (She Writes Press) won the 2018 Independent Publisher Book Award gold medal in social issues. Her first book of poetry is Mortal Beings (Finishing Line Press).

Christopher Watkins lives in Chicago where he is a student in DePaul University's MFA program. His poetry appears in such journals as After Hours, Blueline, and Bosque, among others.

Christopher Woods is a writer and photographer who lives in Chappell Hill, Texas. He has published a novel, The Dream Patch (Corona Publishing.), a prose collection, Under a Riverbed Sky (Panther Creek Press), and a book of stage monologues for actors, Heart Speak (Stone River Press). His photographs can be seen in his gallery, http://christopherwoods.zenfolio.com/. His photography prompt book for writers, From Vision to Text, is forthcoming from Propertius Press.

Terry Wright is an artist and writer whose art has been featured widely in print and digital venues, including Angry Old Man, Chaleur, Full Bleed, Glassworks, Queen Mob's Teahouse, Third Wednesday, and USA Today Exhibitions include the 57th Annual Delta Exhibition. More work on view at cruelanimal.com.

www.ingramcontent.com/pod-product-compliance
Lightning Source LLC
Chambersburg PA
CBHW061105100726
47911CB00012B/408
9781087856391